CREATIVE

TEACHING

IN THE CHURCH

PRENTICE-HALL INTERNATIONAL, INC., *London*
PRENTICE-HALL OF AUSTRALIA, PTY., LTD., *Sydney*
PRENTICE-HALL OF CANADA, LTD., *Toronto*
PRENTICE-HALL FRANCE, S.A.R.L., *Paris*
PRENTICE-HALL OF JAPAN, INC., *Tokyo*
PRENTICE-HALL DE MEXICO, S.A., *Mexico City*

CREATIVE

ELEANOR SHELTON MORRISON

TEACHING

AND

VIRGIL E. FOSTER

IN THE CHURCH

PRENTICE-HALL, INC. Englewood Cliffs, New Jersey

Second printing .... June, 1964

© 1963
PRENTICE-HALL, INC.
Englewood Cliffs, N.J.

Library of Congress Card No.: 63-16578

Printed in the United States of America
19116-C

Introduction

Christian education in Protestant churches has been moving into a period of tremendous change and development. Church school curriculum materials are being redesigned on the basis of research findings and a careful rethinking of the meaning of Christian faith to children and young people. Many of the new Christian education buildings are better arranged, more spacious, and more inviting than most of the older ones. Equipment has been improved. Leadership education has become more imaginative and thorough.

Yet the test of Christian education lies in what happens to children and young people in their homes and local churches. The continued loss of older boys and girls and of young people from many churches indicates that Christian education is not succeeding as it should in bringing children and young people into full participation as committed members. Parents and teachers need to learn how to open to the younger generation the deeper meaning of the church and its faith, so that continuing growth into the Christian community can take place.

The growth of the child and youth population, without a corresponding gain in the number of young-adult and middle-adult teachers, is increasing the responsibility of the available church school leaders. It is extremely important that all parents and church school leaders and officers understand thoroughly the nature of their responsibility and develop leadership skills, wisdom, and devotion in opening to children and young people the doors to meaningful Christian experience.

This book has been written in the hope that it will help parents and church school leaders find joy and a deepening of their own Christian life in sharing their faith with children and young people. The first three chapters deal with the nature of the Christian faith and ways by which it can best be shared. Chapters IV to X describe ways in which this sharing can work out when teachers are imaginative and resourceful in their relations with children and young people of various age-groups. Chapters XI to XVII give suggestions concerning teaching procedures that lend themselves well to the building of meaningful personal relations within groups and to the development of effective learning ventures. There is no attempt to give a blueprint for teaching. The purpose is, rather, to suggest some of the many ways in which learning in the church can become interesting and lead to genuine Christian growth. The aim is to encourage a double-strength teaching, with communication of the Christian message through personal relations and shared experiences as well as through words.

The authors express appreciation to the publishers of the *International Journal of Religious Education* for permission to use in several chapters, with revisions, materials originally published in that magazine.

Contents

Part Two PROCEDURES FOR VARIOUS AGE GROUPS

CREATIVE

TEACHING

IN THE CHURCH

PART ONE

THE FOUNDATION
OF METHOD

NURTURING CHILDREN AND YOUNG PEOPLE IN the Christian faith and life is both an enjoyable and a demanding venture. In sharing the Christian faith, the teacher makes known and interprets God's creative and redemptive love as revealed in Christ and invites the learner to accept fully the life that God has given him. This interpretation and invitation must be given in words and experiences which the children and young people can understand. Furthermore, these must be made meaningful in the life of the teacher and in the relations within the group.

Before a teacher selects procedures to use in any unit of study, he must understand what it is that he and the group need to try to accomplish. What is the faith in which the class is to be nurtured? What are the basic principles of human relations upon which any selection of method is founded? What is his own role in the learning experience of his students?

The three chapters in Part I are directed to these questions. In Chapter I a brief interpretation of the Christian faith and its background in the Bible is given. It is of primary importance that a teacher bring to his teaching an understanding not only of a particular unit being studied, but also of what the Bible as a whole has to say.

In Chapter II is to be found an interpretation of the human relations involved in teaching. Growth comes not only from the teacher's words, but also in what the students learn from each other as they and the teacher try to build a Christian life together. Experiences of love, trust, understanding, forgiveness, and accomplishment, illuminated by informed words, bring a "double-strength" learning.

In Chapter III a further interpretation is given of the teacher's role in this "double-strength" approach to learning. Sharing the Christian faith in life—through the lives of members of the group as well as through the teacher's life—calls for maturity, self-discipline, patience, and an ability to focus on long-range goals more than on incidents of the moment.

These three chapters indicate the kind of thinking about his task and the kind of growth in his own Christian life in which a teacher needs to engage as he leads his group. They indicate the kind of approach to the selection of teaching procedures that a teacher needs to make if his teaching is to be truly creative and fruitful.

Discover the Faith
of the Bible

INTRODUCTION

The Bible is a book of matchless depth and breadth. It places human experience in a perspective that gives meaning to apparently insignificant events. For the Hebrew-Christian community, it has been the unique carrier of the revelation of God to mankind. Indeed, we recognize the activity of God now because his activity in the life of his "chosen people" has been reported in the Bible. We may see in our own lives and in the world about us something of the infinite, the mysterious, the powerful; but in the Bible we have the definitive record of the revelation of the character of God. Our broken and imperfect perceptions of him are clarified by the biblical perspective on God and man.

New light is always breaking forth out of the Bible; a lifetime is too short for discovering all its profound wisdom and meaning. Teachers in the church have no small responsibility, therefore, in helping children and young people to have even the beginning of a personal appreciation of the Bible.

But there is an uneasiness in the minds of some teachers. They know that much of their teaching lacks reality for children and young people. Yet they hesitate to discard the traditional ways of teaching, for fear that their students will then grow up with no knowledge or appreciation of the Bible. Many teachers sense that merely giving children facts about the Bible fails to bring them into dynamic relations with the Creator and Sustainer of life. One new teacher put the dilemma very aptly, "I want to have my teaching be less scaffolding and more building. It seems to me that I spend a great deal of my time with more or less mechanical things, such as the order in which the books of the Bible appear. This is really just scaffolding, which may be necessary temporarily in order that a more permanent building may be constructed. But I feel that only rarely do I get to the real work of helping my students find the living reality of the God to whom the Bible witnesses and thereby discover the meaning of their own lives." This is the "real building" which we hope will be constructed beneath all of the scaffolding.

An outstanding Protestant scholar has said that the Bible is a prompting script for our dialogue with God.[1] This thought emphasizes the fact that teaching the Bible as an end in itself is not our purpose. We are concerned not only that children know about the Bible but that they participate in the life of self-giving love to which it witnesses.

The Bible points beyond itself to the Ground of all being, God. Sometimes we give the impression that we feel our task is complete if students know the names and sequence of the books of the Bible, some selected chapters and verses, and the major stories and events of the Bible. When it is put so baldly, most of us hasten to deny that this is our purpose. But we know that too often our deeds belie our words. We have tended to make an end in itself of teaching the Bible, rather than to keep in mind that the Bible points beyond itself to God. Our teaching task is to introduce children and young people to God at work, as revealed in the Bible, helping them to interpret what happens to them

[1] James Hastings Nichols, *Primer for Protestants* (New York: Association Press, 1951), p. 136.

each day from the perspective of that revelation. Encounter with God, not information about him, is our goal.

Christian teachers need to be sensitive to the pupils and their living so that they and their pupils may probe situations in their lives which the Bible illuminates. This is one of the ways in which Jesus taught. Rarely did he impart information. Rather, he threw the searchlight of God's creative and redemptive love on the dark places of life. He told stories that could take hold in the imaginations of people and grow. He did not ask his disciples to repeat back to him what he had said, with no change due to thinking. He asked that they live it.

The Bible is a powerful resource in helping children and young people come into an increasingly meaningful relation to God, the Creator and Sustainer of their lives. We must find new ways of exposing ourselves and our students to the truth about God and life that the Bible contains. As teachers, we must ask ourselves, "How can I help children and young people experience something of the quality of life portrayed in the Bible? Does this particular approach to teaching increase my students' ability to live more adequately now? How can I make my class a laboratory for experiencing at first hand the meaning of love and concern, as interpreted in the Bible?"

We want to break open the tremendous truth which the Bible contains, that we and our students may taste of it. We will, therefore, always be searching for new ways of discovering more light about the "strange new world within the Bible" as it relates to the strange world within ourselves.

If our effort is to help children and young people discover the way in which the Bible speaks to them personally, we must be ready to accept questions and even doubts about the Bible. Those students who find something impossible or incredible in it are not to be hushed as impertinent or irreverent. Many times, as in ancient Israel, God has spoken out of the ruin of customary religious ways. So it is with doubt. A new spring of truth may come forth from the crack that doubt has made in the encrusted pattern of religious thinking. Doubt is often an evidence of the struggle to understand, and out of the struggle comes new truth. Paul Tillich, the great theologian, has asserted that doubt is always present as an aspect of vital faith.

The Distinctive Character of Biblical Writing

If we are to help children and young people understand the Bible, we need to become acquainted with the distinctive character of its writing. Its language and imagery grow out of the Oriental rather than the Occidental world. The Bible is full of symbolic, picturesque expressions. It is impossible to understand it if these expressions are taken literally.

Hyperbole, metaphor, and vivid imagery are found repeatedly. Tongues of fire rest on people's heads in Acts 2:3. The sun stands still in Joshua 10:13. The spirit comes on Jesus like a dove in Mark 1:10. An ax floats in II Kings 6:4-7. Every hair on a person's head is numbered, according to Matthew 10:30. An ass speaks in Numbers 22:30. A snake speaks in Genesis 3:1-4. Jesus tells of people with logs in their eyes in Matthew 7:3; of people swallowing camels in Matthew 23:24.

These are symbolic ways of expressing truth, and the writers no more intended that they be taken literally than did Jesus intend that we should search for pearls, yeast, and mustard seeds because he compared the Kingdom of Heaven to them.

The figurative, symbolic language of the Bible causes some teachers difficulty in teaching this book. Our matter-of-fact tradition in America, where things are regarded as either true or make-believe, is partly to blame. The tangible and the concrete seem to us more real than the intangible and abstract. Although our religious heritage denies it, our modern mood gives us a lingering suspicion that anything which is not literally true is consequently false. The symbolic seems make-believe and misty. When we approach the Bible, therefore, we have a tendency to feel that, if we cannot interpret it literally as the words are written, then we are denying its validity.

A high school teacher remarked, "I know that the things with which the Bible deals are too big for ordinary language, and that to take the imagery literally is to ruin it. Yet, even as I say that, I feel irreverent. Somehow I have come to believe that the literal conveys more of the real than does the symbolic. I remember my preschooler's attempt to draw a picture of God. I know he cannot do it. I wonder why I insist, therefore, that the biblical pictures of God must be taken literally. They, also, are only a window through which I can glimpse a small portion of God. No words can ever completely capture him."

The fact that a Van Gogh painting is not a literal representation of a landscape does not make it of less worth than a photograph. Because of its distortions and exaggerations, the painting penetrates beneath the surface to the level of feeling and meaning. In order to convey the impression of depth and perspective, the artist has to distort the literal appearance of what he is painting. Yet, in the presence of great art we are aware that something more permanent and deep has been captured than a photograph, in all its literalness, can convey. But the painting's revelation is not seen by the casual passer-by, who laughs and says, "Look at that funny picture of a field!"

The Bible's expressive, symbolic forms also require more than a casual look. To accept them as they appear on the surface is to miss what they really say. For, in speaking of the infinite and the spiritual, one cannot use literal description. Symbolic language is required.

The Bible is not, nor was it ever intended to be, a textbook of history or science. It is concerned with God and his relationship to man. It deals with dimensions of life with which neither history nor science is primarily concerned, such as: life and death, love and hate, justice and injustice, faith and doubt, suffering and joy. These cannot be ground up with a mortar and pestle and analyzed in a laboratory. But they can be understood in the "brilliant indirect light which streams out upon all subsequent history from the incandescent arc of events between the Hebrew patriarchs and the Christian apostles."[2]

A young person, nurtured in the understanding that the Bible does not give a scientific or historical description of the universe, need not discard it as a collection of untruths when it apparently comes into conflict with science or history. He will understand that the Bible is a book about the *meaning* of life rather than about its chronology or anatomy. As William Neil has said, "If the biologist can show us that man developed through millions of years from primitive organisms, well and good. The Bible is more interested in why man is here at all. If the astronomer can lead us to see something more of the wonder of a vast and mysterious universe, let us sit at his feet and listen. The Bible asks us—and the astronomers—why there is a universe for us to marvel at."[3]

The Scope and Variety of the Bible

The Bible has often been called a library of books, with great scope and variety of content. It is essentially that. Although they were written by many different persons over a period of more than seven hundred years, there is a surprising unity in the books of the Bible, concerned as they are with prehistory as well as with historical events dating from the time of Abraham, about 2,000 B.C. The Bible includes poetry, legend, proverb, sermons, stories, biography, letters, conversation, parables, history, prophecy, drama, genealogy, and law. Yet it speaks with amazing singularity to one concern: God's creation of, search for, and redemption of mankind. The wonder is not that there is diversity

---

[2] Walter M. Horton, *Our Christian Faith* (Boston: The Pilgrim Press, 1945), p. xx.

[3] William Neil, *Modern Man Looks at the Bible* (New York: Association Press, 1958), p. 7.

in the Bible, but that in its wholeness it speaks with such consistency of the purpose of God for man.

Some parts of the Bible are of more value to our religious life than are other parts. The Sermon on the Mount is of more value, for example, to children and young people than the book of Nahum. Some parts, such as the genealogies, are of interest to historians but have no relevance in themselves for our life today. Other parts are acutely relevant, but are expressed in language so different from ours that we tend to think of them as relics from the past. The Creation story is an illustration. As an historical or scientific description of the beginnings of the universe, it falls short of what is known by many ten-year-old boys. Yet, the creation story in the Bible is more than a primitive pre-scientific account of the beginning of the universe. It is an affirmation about the meaning of life. It spells the difference between hope and despair, for it affirms that the Creator of the universe is *with* man, not *against* him. It is a powerful and dramatic statement that man is not alone in a hostile universe but is the creation of a God who loves him.

The teacher must study the Bible enough to be able to distinguish those parts of it which have the most relevance to us. In becoming acquainted with the variety of writing in the Bible and with the wide scope of material it includes, we avoid the assumption that a blind opening of the Bible automatically reveals immediate personal guidance. Also, we become more sensitive to the immeasurable richness in the Bible which is available to the disciplined seeker.

What Shall We Teach from the Bible?

There is such a diversity of material in the Bible that we need to distinguish between the parts that are understandable and meaningful to children and young people and those that are not. Unfortunately, some persons assume that all of the Bible—

every page, every sentence, every word—is of equal spiritual and instructional help. This has led in many cases to an indiscriminating use of the Bible, and to confusion and warping of the learner's appreciation of it.

The Bible was written by adults for adults, presupposing mature experience. Some parts are narrative recordings of facts or events, but others communicate profound spiritual insights in symbolic form. If young children are taught stories written to convey a depth of truth beyond their understanding, they are likely to view them as literal narratives of events which happened precisely as the stories say. For instance, many Bible story books for preschool and early elementary-age children include the stories of the Garden of Eden, the Tower of Babel, Noah's Ark, Jonah and the Whale, the Fiery Furnace, Daniel and the Lion's Den, and Lot's wife—all of which communicate meanings beyond the actual story and the child's ability to understand. Preschool and early elementary children see the story as a story; for example, Lot's wife is literally turned to salt. The profound truth that any person's life is immobilized, solidified, deadened, when he looks only to the past, or when he yearns for a return of that which is gone, is subtle and beyond the experience of children whose life is in the present and the future. It is better to save these great symbolic stories for later childhood and adolescence, when the *meaning* can be probed.

There are obvious difficulties in this proposal. Children cannot be wrapped in cellophane; they will hear references to these stories. When they raise questions about them, teachers should be ready to answer out of their own understanding of the Bible. But it is probably best not to include these stories intentionally until late childhood or adolescence. Often it is difficult to reinterpret a story if it has been accepted as literally true. Each teacher must ask himself why he wants to teach any given story. Is it understandable to the pupils whom he is teaching? Is it being taught only so that they will be acquainted with this story?

At what age might it be more appropriately taught? Does it help illuminate the present life of the student? Does it aid in developing a growing relation to God?

What understanding of the nature of God does a particular selection of Scripture convey? Sometimes—as in several of the Psalms and parts of the Pentateuch—the fierce patriotism of the writers led them to picture him in terms that might be used of a tribal war-god. Other parts of the Old Testament reflect a period in Jewish history when the emphasis was on legal niceties of religious observance, and good fortune was equated with God's favor. Christ and many of the prophets, on the other hand, insisted that God's love includes enemies, and that suffering is not an indication of God's displeasure. Indeed, in suffering for other persons one can demonstrate God's way of working in the world.

In order to teach the Bible effectively, one must understand the abilities of his students. It is very difficult for young children to grasp historical sequence and geographical references. Usually the public schools do not attempt to teach history and geography until about the fourth grade. Since meaningful teaching of much of the Bible is dependent on some appreciation of its historical and geographical setting, the church can profit by being aware of the practices of its public school at this point. Although very small children have some sense of fairness, it is at the junior age that the sense of justice becomes developed. Therefore, juniors and junior highs can appreciate biblical passages about justice more than young children can.

Parts of the Bible that are out of keeping with Jesus' spirit and his understanding of God are not suitable for teaching to children. Jesus' largeness of vision, his depth of concern for persons, his emphasis on the inwardness of the religious life, his single-minded devotion to the will of a righteous and loving Father—these are criteria for selection of biblical material for children.

Even with the life and teachings of Jesus, we use discrimination. We do not, for instance, start with the crucifixion and resurrection in the early years of childhood, nor with the nature miracles and apocalyptic sayings. Some parts of the New Testament are difficult even for scholars to interpret. With the New Testament, as with the Old Testament, the primary concern is that the passages chosen have meaning for the child or young person *now*.

The Unique Revelation of the Bible

The Bible is unique in religious literature because it is a record, not of abstract principles or ideals, but of the life of a particular people and the revelation therein of the Creator of all men. The specific nature of the Bible sets it apart from other religious literature: it deals with a specific nation (the Jews), a specific man (Jesus Christ), and another specific people (the Christian community).

This specific quality is what makes the Bible so strangely relevant to all men of all time. It has *universal* meaning because it is the record of the rebellion and faith, apostasy and trust, failure and vision, of a *specific* people. How can this be? In the same way that a case study of one boy can throw light on the nature of all the boys. More wisdom is gained by looking at a slice of life than by theorizing about life in the abstract. The Bible takes a slice of history and asserts that in it all men find the meaning of their lives and of the universe.

The Bible uses history—that is, everyday life—as the setting for the drama of God and man. God is found, not on a far-off Mount Olympus, but in and through the events of everyday existence. It was out of their own experiences that the Hebrew people came to know God. The Bible is, therefore, not a book of moral laws or wise sayings, predominantly, but an account of the way in which the Hebrews perceived the activity of God in the events of the life of their nation. The wise sayings and teachings grew out of the Hebrew interpretation of God at work in their lives. Event and interpretation are intertwined and integral to each other—all the way from the exodus out of Egypt to the crucifixion. The event alone might or might not have been significant, but as the channel of the activity of the everlasting God it became freighted with tremendous meaning. Modern man, viewing his life in the light of these events of the Bible, may come to a radically new outlook on his life as the arena for God's activity today.

Bernhard Anderson[4] has characterized the Bible as a drama. Although such a description is somewhat artificial because not all parts of the Bible fit into the scheme of drama, it is helpful in organizing an otherwise confusing mass of material.

A drama uses events and action as the medium through which its truth is communicated. A play about family life, for instance, is quite different in form from an essay about family life. The communication of the play is indirect, filtering through the action and events on the stage. One must *think* about a truly great play in order to determine precisely what it means; and its meaning becomes available only to those who are willing to wrestle with what they have seen. So it is with the Bible. The activity of God in the events of ordinary life—in biblical or contemporary times— is hidden except to those who have the "eyes of faith."

If the Bible is drama, it must have several acts, a beginning and an end. What is this drama?*

THE PROLOGUE. *In the Beginning, God.* The Bible opens with a prologue which states the nature of what is to follow. It spells out the direction which the drama is to take. "In the beginning God" and "Man rebelled and took things into his own hands"— these are the two themes introduced in the prologue.

ACT I. *The Exodus.* The deliverance of the Jews out of Egypt, a minor event in world history, became the crucial event for the

---

[4] Bernhard W. Anderson, *The Unfolding Drama of the Bible* (New York: Association Press, 1955).

* The authors are indebted to Dr. Bernhard Anderson for the basic framework of the following interpretation.

Hebrew people because they found in it an encounter with the living God. Because of the exodus, they felt that they were to have a unique relationship to God and to his work in the world. God needed them as a people who could demonstrate what it meant to know and worship the Creator of the universe. In his loving-kindness and grace, he chose to deliver them. They felt that their deliverance symbolized God's calling them to be a people who could embody in their personal and national life the difference that God makes.

ACT II. *The Covenant.* The Hebrews entered into a covenant with God which was the basic framework of their religious life. It was a contract with the living God—not with some far-off deity to be sought, but with a present Lord who was seeking out man, searching for ways in which he and man could be related. This portion of the drama is a drastic departure from the practices of the times. Surrounding religions did not emphasize the quality of relations between man and man as having anything to do with religious rites. Middle East religions were based on fertility cults aimed at producing good crops and abundant families, and the placation of the gods was their purpose.

The Hebrew people, once they had entered Palestine, tended to practice some of the rites of their neighbors. Yet, their prophets continually reminded them that their covenant with God demanded an upright and ethical quality in their lives and was not primarily concerned with religious rites in the temple.

There was laid upon them, the people chosen by God, a special responsibility. Their treatment of their brother, their neighbor, the stranger, the oppressed, became the major avenue by which they fulfilled their destiny as a people of God. Not through ritual, but through living brotherliness would the world come to know the God of Abraham, Isaac, and Jacob.

ACT III. *The Chastisement of God.* Failing to fulfill this high destiny, the Hebrew people felt the chastisement of God. Many peoples have been taken captive or have been subjugated. But the prophets of Israel saw God's action in their nation's exile and captivity: his disciplining of the people whose failure to live justly he could not tolerate. In the disintegration of their nation was seen God's judgment on those whom he loved and of whom he expected much.

The demand for just living, then, was not an abstract teaching or commandment, but a requirement known and violated in day-to-day associations. The prophets gazed, not into a crystal ball, but into the life of their nation, and saw there the activity of God and the failure of His people.

ACT IV. *A New Meaning in Suffering.* Shattered as a nation, bent under the heel of a foreign power, separated from their homeland, the Hebrews began to perceive, through their eloquent spokesman, Deutero (Second) Isaiah, that faithfulness to God does not always bring material success. Suffering might be not only a discipline, but a means by which they could reveal the deepest nature of God. If they were able to take on themselves in their suffering the consequences of other nations' wrongs, this act might help people to understand the activity of God. Not by mighty displays of prowess would they show the real nature of God, but by an identification with others so deep that they took on themselves the consequences of the misdeeds of those others. It was to a mission of suffering love that they were called in their covenant with the eternal God. As he had delivered them from Egypt, so God would deliver them from this captivity, but this time with a greater purpose than to establish them as a nation. This time they must be a light to all the nations.

ACT V. *The Climax, Jesus Christ.* The Hebrew people failed to be able to live up to their mission, and once again God revealed himself and his purpose to man. He came to man, not in some supernatural display, but in and through the events of ordinary existence. He came in the form of a man—incarnate—taking on human flesh and form.

How much more appropriate it might have seemed if God had

chosen to reveal himself in a Caesar rather than a carpenter. Should not the emissary of God come with panoply befitting his mission, rather than as one who was to minister? How much more clearly the might and majesty of God might have been revealed if the carpenter had not gotten himself killed! But, once again, God was patiently trying to show the true nature of the godly life and of his intention for mankind.

ACT VI. *A New Community.* The new Christian community now became the carrier of God's good news for mankind. In the life of the followers of Christ, the Bible asserts, is to be found the continuing incarnation of Christ. The church is his body. Its mission is to show forth to all men the new life to be had through Jesus Christ.

EPILOGUE. *The Lord God Omnipotent Reigneth.* The ending of the drama reasserts the supremacy of the one eternal God. He is the Creator and Sustainer of the universe, and he will be the meaning at the end.

In oversimplified form, this is the drama of the Bible. At every point it has its roots, not in blinding revelations handed down from on high, but in the events of the life of a people, a man, and a nation. Charles Duell Kean[5] has pictured the drama of the Bible as an hourglass turned on its side: first, the people of Israel (the base), narrowing to one man, then widening again to the people of the Way—these are the carriers of God's word to mankind.

God at Work in Our Lives

It is impossible to prescribe the way in which God may become real to a teacher through the Bible. The very process of teaching, however, often causes a crystallization of one's own ideas. How often has a teacher remarked, "I am not sure what

[5] Charles Duell Kean, *God's Word to His People* (Philadelphia: The Westminster Press, 1956), p. 186.

the children (or young people) are learning, but I am certainly learning a lot!"

This learning must go beyond the intellectual process of understanding the Bible to a "stance of faith." As I read the Bible, I see in Adam my own rebellion and egoism; in Eve, my tendency to blame others; in Cain, my anger when my efforts are rejected; in Israel of Amos' day, my giving of inordinate amounts of time to trivial matters; in the Pharisees, my tendency to feel myself in the right and others in the wrong; in the crucifixion mob, my fear of stepping out of line with what others are doing.

I also echo the Psalmist's conviction that God's mercy is everlasting; Job's defiant assertion, "Though he slay me, yet will I trust him"; Paul's undaunted certainty that nothing can separate us from the love of God in Christ Jesus. As I perceive the "I" in the Bible, it ceases to be remote history, speculation, or catechism, with little meaning in my life.

Alan Richardson, in his provocative little book, *A Preface to Bible Study*, spells out a new interpretation of the meaning of the inspiration of the Scriptures which is pertinent. He says that the inspiration of the Bible has to do not so much with whether God dictated every word of it, as whether there is something in it which is true for us personally. It is not concerned so much with whether the words of the Bible are infallible as with whether the Bible speaks pertinently to me. "We must discover that God has spoken a message to mankind, and that he intended it for us. In the proper Christian sense of the term, the meaning of the inspiration of the Scripture for me is that I recognize that God's message has been sent into the world with my name and address on it."[6]

The Bible, faithfully and carefully studied, helps me to see the way in which God speaks to me *today* in my daily experience. Our purpose in teaching the Bible is to make this remarkable

[6] Alan Richardson, *A Preface to Bible Study* (Philadelphia: The Westminster Press, 1944), p. 38.

discovery for ourselves, and then try to help children and young people discover it.

The life of faith is not one of believing "what you know ain't so." It is trusting that the most real things in life are goodness, truth, and love, not evil, falsehood, and hate. It is the willingness to try (and fail) and try again the new way of creative love. It is the affirmation that the life which makes this venture will be supported by that power we know as God.

In each situation, I have the choice of shrinking back to yesterday's patterns, of remaining frozen where I am, or of venturing out into an uncharted course of action.[7] The God who revealed himself in the events of the lives of the Hebrew people will reveal himself in the events of my life. He will not bludgeon his way in by knocking down the doors of my life. I can shut him out by shrinking back; this is essentially what lack of faith is. Or I can know him as I venture into new realms of experience; this is faith in action—trust which allows me to move ahead without complete knowledge of the outcome ahead of time.

As I meet each new crisis or responsibility, there is the possibility of a redemptive meeting with God. He is there, if I have the openness to perceive him; he is there, bidding me to launch forth into a fuller life.

How Did the Master Teacher Deal with Persons?

Although Jesus was steeped in the religious heritage of the Hebrews and quoted the Scriptures, he interpreted God and his Kingdom in terms of familiar experiences. He did not, so far as is recorded, "teach" the Bible, except in his appearances in the synagogue to read and expound the Scriptures. Most of his time was spent out among the people, bearing witness to the Reality to Whom the Scriptures point.

[7] For further development of these ideas, see Lewis Joseph Sherrill, *The Struggle of the Soul* (New York: The Macmillan Company, 1958).

He spoke of bread and stones, of fish and nets, of coins and houses, of seeds and lamps, of salt and yeast, of wine and weddings, of flowers and storms. No one could accuse Jesus of failing to have the Bible as his textbook, but he taught in many ways. He brought new meaning to the law and prophets (fulfilled them), and also to the Psalms.

It was in face-to-face relations that Jesus did most of his teaching. He saw the real self beneath the masks which people wore, and he nurtured it into flower. Through the vigor of his trust, he inspired people who had limped along in life for years to step out with new buoyancy. He saw possibilities within people who had been termed hopeless by others, and he believed them into new life. He saw persons splitting apart, and, through his faith in them, he helped them to become whole again.

This man, Jesus Christ, was and is God's Word to us. His life and death, his words and teachings, were the medium God used to communicate with us. We must meditate deeply about ourselves and our teaching to be sure that we are allowing God to use us in his contemporary communication.

How well do we let God speak through us if we favor children who know all the answers and ignore those who are inarticulate? How well do we reveal God if we let subtle cruelties and cliques operate unchallenged in our class? How does God speak through us when we make children and young people feel that accidents and mistakes are irreparable, and that they can be forgiven only slowly, if at all?

By what standards do we measure the success of our class? Is it successful if a member of the group can quote a Bible verse when his parents ask, "What did you learn this morning?" Or is it more successful if a student, almost without knowing it, has developed a genuine concern for another person, an ability to see the weakness of another and still accept and love him?

The Master Teacher yearned for each person to know and commit himself to God, the loving and righteous Father. In this effort, he expostulated less than he demonstrated.

Making the Bible Meaningful to Children and Young People

Often the Bible is taught on the assumption that it will be useful to students in the future, even though they do not understand at present what they are learning. Yet no one would try to teach kindergarten boys to be Boy Scouts. One cannot be a Boy Scout until he is eleven years old. That is the appropriate time to learn the Scout law and the requirements for Scout activities. Memorizing them six years earlier in an effort to prepare for Scouting would be meaningless.

It is in the adequate living of the present that a person is prepared to live in the future. The real task of the Christian teacher, then, is to find those concerns and needs that are important in the present life of a child or youth, and to seek ways in which the Bible can illuminate and reshape them.

Premature teaching of isolated sections of the Bible that have little or no present meaning to children and young people may result in an impression that the Bible is "all right for preachers, but impractical for me." The Bible throws a blinding light on our pettiness, our false values, our self-centeredness, while at the same time lighting the way that leads to largeness of living, concern with what is true, and selfless love. The combination of illumination and judgment in the Bible makes it an acutely relevant document, but one from which we continually try to hide. Let it not be said that teachers abet the escape from the truth of the Bible by making it appear to be a jumble of meaningless words and happenings. Let it be said, rather, that teachers, in a serious and continuing fashion, have helped children and young people find the relation between the Bible and their present living.

What do we mean by the real concerns of children and young people? Not the things they might mention if asked, "What are you most interested in right now?" These would probably include sports, airplanes, hobbies, animals, and (in the case of adolescents) clothes and popularity. These are actually the changing and ephemeral concerns of children and young people. The basic concerns and needs are much more profound (and often unknown or unarticulated by the person involved), affecting the way a person feels about himself, others, and the universe about him, determining his fears, angers, hopes, and dreams. These latter are the real concerns of childhood and youth to which the Bible speaks, because these are the matters with which the Bible deals. The teacher, then, must know what some of these needs and concerns are in general for the age level at which he is teaching. In addition, through careful observation, conversation, and sensitive listening, he must attempt to discover those tasks which are unique to each student. In one case, it may be the need to find that he can do something on his own; in another, it may be learning to deal with hostile and resentful feelings; in another, it may be discovering that he is a person of worth in his own eyes and in the eyes of others. The person who fails in childhood and adolescence to find adequate ways of dealing with these basic needs and concerns has to continue fighting with them into adulthood. If he does not achieve in childhood a sense of his own dignity, he may feel the need to fight for esteem and attention in every situation, or he may run from any situation that demands something from him.

W. B. J. Martin, an English clergyman and writer, says, "If the Bible is not an interpreter of life, leave it alone; if it doesn't have anything to say to life, forget it!"[8] The teacher must constantly ask himself, "What is the task that this particular child needs most to accomplish *now* in his living? Can I assist in the develop-

[8] W. B. J. Martin, unpublished speech given at Chicago Theological Seminary, January 1958.

ment of a relationship between this child and the living God revealed in the Bible? What parts of the Bible are most meaningful and relevant for this person? How can I be an interpreter of the Bible to him?"

Many adults have found in the Bible resources of tremendous inspiration. Some of them insist that these are available to them in times of crisis because they memorized them, meaningful or not, when they were children. It is more probable that they are available because they have been relearned many times since childhood in situations in which they were pertinent and meaningful.

The Most Powerful Communication Is Nonverbal

Although the Bible is often referred to as the *Word of God*, this does not imply that it is a transcript of God's verbal communication to man. Rather, the term refers to the transcending purpose of God, which predates the written words of the Bible, and which is continually above and beyond the actual word of the Bible. Most often, God's biblical communication to man comes through an event (such as deliverance from bondage), a series of events (such as those leading to the decadence of Israel, culminating in the Exile), or through illumination due to an event (such as that in Hosea's encounter with God in the infidelity of his wife). Supremely, God's Word came to mankind in the event of Jesus Christ. The life and death of Jesus, even more than his teachings, were the Word of God to mankind—the clue to the mystery of the meaning of living. It was what Jesus was and did, even more than what he said, that made him the Word of God.

If this is the nature of biblical communication, then teaching the Bible involves more than teaching words—it is the conveying of the Word of good news behind the words of the Bible. This we can do most effectively by enacting it as well as by talking about it.

Nonverbal communication is far more powerful than verbal communication. The understanding look, the sympathetic touch of a hand, the clenched fist, convey a world of wordless meaning. Even the smallest child participates in this kind of communication. He can experience trust, understanding, mutuality, forgiveness. All of these a child can know without hearing a word about them.

Teachers need to understand that their nonverbal communication is as important as their verbal communication. They must be some of the "chosen people" of this century, chosen to demonstrate through their lives what is God's way for men. This demonstration takes place not so much by talking about the Bible as by expressing love in our human relations. Moses protested to the Lord that he, of all people, was unworthy of leading his people— he could not even speak well. Too often teachers have assumed that the major qualification for teaching is the ability to articulate one's faith—to speak well. This ability is important, but of even greater importance is the ability to bring into one's associations with children and young people the unswerving concern, the trust, the challenging demand, and the loving acceptance which we know in fellowship with God.

Our goal is to have children and young people come into a trustful relation with the One who sustains us all. We must see to it, then, that they are treated in our classes in such a way that they feel they can trust themselves and others. If a child cannot trust either himself or others, it is unlikely that he will have a trustful relation to God.

Ours is the task of translating the reconciling love let loose in the world through Jesus Christ into the relations in our classrooms. The graciousness of the Eternal, who sees shortcomings yet bestows unconditional love, must be ours toward every member of the group, even the most obstreperous and unlovable. Each one must come to see that he is looked on, not as a blot on the landscape, but as a person with great possibilities and needs. If we believe that God is love and that our job as teachers is to help children and young people understand that, then we will love!

As Harvey C. Cox has said,

> . . . we communicate biblical truth in the realm of . . . personal relations by being, not by talking. In the Easter event, God's reconciling act defeats separation and fear and insecurity. "Christ hath conquered sin and death." Our witness to that faith is not to talk about it but to be it. This implies that we be the means by which men and women are freed from the things that terrify them: being unneeded, unwanted, unnoticed. . . . In theological jargon, one might say, "the life of the biblical God, known to us in Christ, is poured out in the act of reconciling men to each other and, thus, to himself." We make known (communicate) the truth of this God by enacting in our lives his patient, untiring efforts toward reconciliation. The words are distinctly secondary. Like the words of the Bible, which but give witness to the "mighty acts of God," our words merely point in humility to what God is doing for men. They invite the hearer's response, not to our words, but to God's action.[9]

BIBLIOGRAPHY

The Abingdon Bible Commentary. New York: Abingdon Press.

Anderson, Bernhard W., *The Unfolding Drama of the Bible.* New York: Association Press, 1955.

————, *Rediscovering the Bible.* New York: Association Press, 1951.

Brown, Robert McAfee, *The Bible Speaks to You.* Philadelphia: The Westminster Press, 1955.

Cox, Harvey C., *The Bible, the Church, the Student Christian Move-*

[9] Harvey C. Cox, "Religion, Sex, and Politics," *The Intercollegian,* October 1959, p. 18.

ment. New York: The United Student Christian Council, 475 Riverside Drive.

Harkness, Georgia, *Toward Understanding the Bible.* Nashville: Methodist Publication Society, 1952.

The Harpers Commentary Series. New York: Harper and Row, 1960.

Horton, Walter M., *Our Christian Faith.* Boston: The Pilgrim Press, 1945.

The Interpreter's Bible in Twelve Volumes. New York: Abingdon Press, 1952.

Kean, Charles Duell, *God's Word to His People.* Philadelphia: The Westminster Press, 1956.

The Moffatt Commentary Series. New York: Harper and Row.

Neil, William, *Modern Man Looks at the Bible.* New York: Association Press, 1958.

————, *The Rediscovery of the Bible.* New York: Harper and Row, 1954.

Nichols, James Hastings, *Primer for Protestants.* New York: Association Press, 1951.

Richardson, Alan, *A Preface to Bible Study.* Philadelphia: The Westminster Press, 1944.

Sherrill, Lewis Joseph, *The Gift of Power.* New York: The Macmillan Company, 1955.

————, *The Struggle of the Soul.* New York: The Macmillan Company, 1958.

Wright, Ernest G., and Reginald H. Fuller, *The Book of the Acts of God.* New York: Doubleday and Co., 1957.

Wygal, Winifred, and Harold B. Ingalls, *Deep Are the Sources.* New York: Association Press, 1947.

II

Double-Strength Teaching

A child or young person needs to belong to a group that demonstrates the distinctive quality of Christian living. When the Christian faith is expressed in the life of a group, it is possible to have a "double-strength" teaching, through experience and through verbal interpretation.

Since God is known in the events of everyday life, it is our concern as teachers that the part of everyday life represented in our classrooms be an avenue of God's activity, not a roadblock.

Love must have a community in which it is nourished. A church school class can be that community for children and young people before they are able to participate fully in the larger life of the church. It can be if the conditions are created which allow loving and concerned persons to emerge.

We know some of these conditions, and we must search always for new understanding of how Christian persons develop. One of the conditions, for example, is that we recognize that all persons are of worth and must be respected as sons of God. The feelings, ideas, fears and hopes of each are as important as those of the teacher and are to be treated with respect, even when they are negative or hostile.

We know, also, that love is the key to understanding the nature of God and is the way to human fulfillment. Therefore, we shall try to surround children and young people with a supportive group life that frees them from constricting fear, guilt, and self-preoccupation, so that they can love others. We shall try to learn what it means to be the fellowship of the forgiving and the forgiven. Since we want young Christians to be able increasingly to love their neighbors as themselves, we shall provide opportunities for listening to the other person, trying out how it feels to be in another's position, and seeing things as he sees them.

If we are to provide the climate in which the biblical faith can take root and grow, we must understand how that faith can find expression in group life. Let us look at some aspects of the Christian life to see their implications for teaching and learning within a group. Then we can consider some procedures that are consistent with the practice of the Christian faith.

DISTINCTIVE CHARACTERISTICS OF THE CHRISTIAN LIFE

1. It Is an Interdependent Life

It is impossible to be a Christian all by oneself. It is in human relations that we discover who we are, who God is, and how he works. Paul's characterization of the Christian community as the "Body of Christ" is an audacious statement of the fact that in the gathered company of Christians the spirit of Christ becomes incarnate, creating a loving, reconciling fellowship. A class can be for its members a microcosm of the church rather than only an age-group subdivision.

Carroll A. Wise, in *Psychiatry and the Bible,* says that in the Christian community or fellowship,

Each has a responsibility to the others, but this responsibility is not motivated by legalistic requirements, but by freedom in the kind of love which creates mutual helpfulness. . . . The New Testament does not teach that men should become so absorbed in God nor in conformity to a group that they lose their identity as persons. Rather they find completion of their personal identity through participation in the life of God and of their fellow men. . . . Fellowship is essential for health; isolation leads to illness in one form or another. In fostering the experience of Christian community, the Church provides a foundation for the development of wholesome, mature persons.[1]

A high-school senior recently said,

You know, most young people my age aren't very courageous when it comes to being different. We want very much for others to like us, so we go along with their ideas. This year, for the first time, I have found the courage to be different, and I'm sure this courage comes from my belonging to the youth fellowship at the church. Now I dare to be different from the "neat guys" at school, because I know there are others who feel the same as I do. We don't have any big crusade or anything; we just refuse to cheat and to go along with certain dating practices. Probably we are called "odd balls," but I'd rather be an "odd ball" than "ball up" my life forever. All by myself I could not have done this, but having talked with other young people at church, and knowing that we sort of stand together, makes me a lot stronger.

Participation in a group that has a sense of where it is going, what it stands for, and what it stands against, produces persons who are willing to act in ways that would not be possible for them as lone individuals. In the Christian fellowship, members feel that they are involved in an enterprise of tremendous importance, in which they need and depend on each other; and they develop distinctive ways of thinking, relating, and living.

If it becomes one of the purposes of a class to work actively at becoming a supporting fellowship for its members, a society of

[1] Carroll A. Wise, *Psychiatry and the Bible* (New York: Harper and Row, Publishers, Incorporated, 1956), pp. 127, 128, 129.

brothers, much of the good news of the reconciliation of Christianity can be communicated in the life of the group as well as in its study. The class may become a "burning bush"—a meeting place between God and ourselves.

2. Every Person Is Recognized as Having Infinite Worth

Created in the image of God, no human being can be treated as a tool or a thing. He has, potentially if not presently, some of the capabilities which his Creator possesses infinitely: he is able to love and receive love, to suffer and identify with others in their suffering, to imagine and to create, to make decisions and to carry through purposes.

This means that a teacher will recognize each child or young person as one of infinite worth. He will see in each the image of God, and love him as a child of God despite all the distortions of that image. Each person will be encouraged to be himself in all his uniqueness without feeling that he has to be like anyone else in order to find acceptance. The atmosphere in the class will say to each member: "You are wanted here; you are needed. You are a significant and acceptable member of the group." The teacher will help members of the group become aware of their own behavior that makes others feel insignificant, or conversely that makes them feel of worth.

The teacher's goal is not to "reform" members of a group, but to extend to them such concern and understanding that they will be able to change themselves. It is impossible to change another person; the most fruitful act is to love the other, leaving him to do his own changing, with the help of God.

A teacher will make a genuine effort to understand the concerns of each member of the group—how he feels about himself and others, what delights or distresses him. In coming to this kind of relation with each person, the teacher may have to discard notions about what is proper in speech, dress, and manners for children and young people; otherwise, he may remain a stranger outside their world, never getting to know them.

A mother of a fourth-grade boy tells of a remarkable teacher-pupil relationship:

> One day I was at school, waiting outside, when I saw my son waggling his hands, sticking out his tongue, and yelling at his teacher. I was about to restrain him when I saw her standing in the window sticking out her tongue at him.
>
> As the year went on, I discovered that a part of Mrs. R's uniqueness was her genuineness in responding to children. She was not afraid to appear undignified, yet there was never a moment when the children forgot that she was an adult and they children. They respected her more than any teacher they ever had. They vied with each other to do things for her. She was neither kittenish nor kiddish, but had a vital quality to which the children responded.
>
> On registration day the room was crowded with her previous year's students coming by to visit with her. She was able to reveal herself and her own dreams and disappointments to an amazing degree. I would have been afraid to tell fourth-graders about my childhood and my present life, for fear they would be bored or amused. She sensed that self-revelation is a part of a genuine relationship, so she shared memories of her childhood in Italy, and daily experiences with her four-year-old.
>
> She elicited similar sharing by the children. They told her things they probably never told another adult. The most remarkable thing was the way she combined all these personal qualities with an ability to motivate the pupils to learn. She used their interests and abilities. John was in succession a member of the star committee, the games-from-many-lands committee, the amphibious-animal committee, and many others. He ransacked the house for material for his committee. Never before had I seen him not only interested in his school work but willing to admit to other persons that it was interesting.
>
> When Mrs. R. moved away last summer, it was a personal loss for the children. She has written letters to each of the children, and if John is typical, the letters are treasured. She made a lasting impression; and it was not a personal empire she built around herself. She saw each of them a human being worth

responding to and working with, a person of real value. Through her belief in them she enabled the children to do more than they had ever done before.

This report reveals the dramatic effect of an atmosphere of acceptance and warmth in a class. In contrast, children and young people are dwarfed by coldness, lack of acceptance, threat, and competition.

A teacher has a great deal to do with this atmosphere, and the arrangement of the room has a bearing. Informality in seating and speaking, abolishing the need for hand-raising, and allowing freedom of movement—all help to create an environment in which teacher can respond to pupil and pupil respond to pupil in a person-valuing way.

The teacher will provide opportunities for children or young people to assume real responsibility (not mere busy work), so that they may see themselves as important and needed. A junior-high boy, who had participated in a project to earn money for sending a goat to a country in Southeast Asia, later said to his teacher, "When are we going to do something *real* again?"

Some things a teacher will do in order to provide experiences that dramatize the value of every individual. There are also things he will refuse to do because they are inconsistent with his goal. The use of competition and ridicule does not reinforce Christian growth. Competition may be a form of motivation necessary in some parts of our common life, but it is not necessary in Christian education. Those who achieve competitively are on guard lest someone unseat them. Competition sets each person against every other person, as a rival to be beaten rather than as a partner with whom to collaborate. It makes him suspicious, uneasy, and insensitive, eager to be superior to others rather than to help them. It drowns his concern for those who are unable to keep up. It creates an atmosphere of isolation, pressure, and uneasiness rather than one of warm fellowship and Christian love.

Ridicule and sarcasm, also, are incompatible with the Christian view that each person is of value. Feeling isolated by being laughed at is an experience which few of us can endure. It withers self-respect. A teacher may find that by talking sarcastically to a disturbing member of the group he can isolate the person and cause the rest of the class to reject him and his behavior. He may also discover that children and young people trained in ridicule can turn their weapons on anyone, including the teacher. Ridicule makes a person unable to be his best self, for he is uneasy and uncertain about where he stands.

3. It Is a Life of Trust

The roll call of faith in the eleventh chapter of the Letter to the Hebrews is an account of persons who trusted and ventured. "By faith Abraham . . . went out, not knowing where he was to go." He and many others did not wait until their action was proved right beyond a doubt, but went out in faith, validating their trust in action.

We continually confront God in situations in which we must move ahead before all the facts are in or must shrink back into accustomed paths. The trusting person acts on the assumption, not completely proved, that love is stronger than hate, that the creative and redemptive powers in life are more powerful than the destructive ones.

The roots of trust go back to infancy. A child learns early whether he must proceed cautiously, protecting himself against possible hurt and betrayal, or is safe in responding to others in love. If he finds himself considered worthy and acceptable, he finds others worthy and acceptable. Self-respect and self-acceptance are not sinful. They make one able to see his own faults and abilities honestly, and to pass on to the task of bringing God's loving concern to other human beings. When the innermost self becomes strong enough to exist without being pampered and accorded first place, the person is free to care for others, helping them to become the kinds of persons they are intended to be.

The small child begins to trust himself as he discovers that he can do something competently—button his coat, water a plant, feed himself, or paint a picture. Finding himself adequate in these matters, he is free to venture into other areas with confidence.

Children and young people come to the church with widely varying degrees of trust in themselves and others. All come, however, needing to find themselves in new relations of trust. Their teachers, with the help of parents if possible, will try to provide children the surroundings that enable them to trust themselves and others and to build dependable, consistent, and faithful associations with each other.

The ability to trust God is interwoven with the ability to trust oneself and his fellows. One who has experienced little consistency in the behavior of other people may have difficulty knowing when to trust God and when to proceed with caution or doubt. The person who has learned from experience that other persons must be distrusted will have difficulty in feeling that life is basically trustworthy. He will find it hard to risk revealing himself to others in trust.

The attitude of the teacher is of primary importance in helping pupils grow in the ability to respond trustfully to life. Seemingly insignificant things are important: the teacher's commitment to be present consistently; rules for the class that are sympathetically but consistently maintained, so that the same act is not unnoticed one Sunday and punished the next; the outlawing of ridicule; encouragement to the group to try new things and to accept failure as a part of trying.

The teacher needs to understand that the willingness to risk oneself in relations of trust grows slowly and out of continued experience with the same persons. Therefore, he will find many opportunities for the group to be together. Since a church group must be one in which the weak are supported and encouraged, rather than ignored or ridiculed, he will maintain an unswerving attitude of good will and expectant encouragement toward each pupil. Thoughtful concern will be extended to withdrawn or rebellious members, as well as to the responsive and compliant ones. The teacher will continually examine his attitudes and procedures to be sure that they are helping, not hindering, children and young people to grow in that aspect of Christian faith which is trust.

A sophomore church membership class had met together for sixteen sessions. The emphasis had been on personal response to the material being discussed. In the midst of a discussion about evidences of the existence of God, a boy said, "This is O.K., but when are we going to get to the heart of the matter, where we really are? I want to know how I can change."

Quick glances shot around the room, but no one smiled. He continued, "I know I am supposed to be one of the 'neat crowd' at school, but I am not living the way I really want to. I keep doing what I don't want to do."

The teacher listened as he talked further. Two girls soon admitted that they felt discouraged about themselves and did not know what to do. They were among the leaders of the sophomore class, suave, self-assured, not given to public confession.

Later one of the girls said to the teacher, "I think that this is the only place where we are not afraid to admit that we don't know everything." An atmosphere of warmth and trust had been established over a period of weeks, so that it was possible to reveal the troubling, private sore spots in individual lives without fear of being ignored or ridiculed.

4. It Is a Life of Love

The heart of the Christian good news is that God loves us, despite our failures and unworthiness. He accepts us as we are and welcomes us back when we have fallen short and are ready to recognize our failure. This good news gives us the motivation to love others: "We love because he first loved us."

The Old and New Testaments point to the inseparability of love for God and love for brother. A striking passage (I John 4:20) says that anyone who says he loves God, and hates his brother, is a liar. The prophets spelled out the nature of religious living: to love God humbly, and to demonstrate by a merciful and just life that one loves his fellow men. Jesus summed up the law and the prophets by tying together the commandments to love God and to love our neighbors.

In teaching the biblical faith, we seek to help children and young people learn to love other persons and accept their love, as well as to love God and accept his love. It is our purpose to help them know the "full round of love," as Ross Snyder puts it.

> Love is "putting on our neighbor." By "putting on our neighbor" is meant that we stand *within* the feelings and thoughts, the anger, evil, and frustrations, the joys and triumphs, of those near us—they are not alien to us; we are not just external observers. And also, all our strength, understanding, and resources are available to him. And it is done without demanding "that for this," or creating dependency.[2]

Loving another person involves being concerned for him, actively working so that he will know an abundant life. Love is not dependent on the lovableness or attractiveness of the person loved, but on his need for that love. It involves respect for him as a unique person and response to him in his uniqueness, coupled with a willingness to risk being hurt by his rejection or betrayal of love.

If we are to help children and young people love God and their brothers, we must provide the "double-strength" teaching in

---

[2] Ross Snyder, "Religious Living with Three and Four-Year-Olds; What is the Living?" *The Chicago Theological Seminary Register*, Volume XLVIII, Number 1, January 1953, p. 4.

which members of the class not only discuss the meaning of love but experience it.

The teacher's willingness and ability to accept members of the group *as they are* is crucial. He will not think of them as "good" or "bad," but will try to understand why they are as they are and what they are trying to become. His goal will be to learn how to extend unconditional love to each person. He will demonstrate that each is cherished and treasured as he is, that he does not have to be or think a certain way to find favor. A pupil given such genuine love and acceptance is able to become a different kind of person more quickly than one who is reprimanded, scolded, and admonished to be "good."

Jesus did not command us to discipline little children, but to accept them. He did not say, "Teach one another a lesson," but "Love one another." Children and young people sense immediately when they are with an adult who respects them genuinely. Such an adult has the initial requirements for being a Christian teacher.

Love is not simply a feeling of kindness toward everyone. It looks squarely at failures as well as successes. It recognizes the ways a person acts in spite of himself, driven by previous experience and by his feelings about himself and others. Love helps a person to be aware of who he is and who he wants to become, and to accept responsibility for his own behavior, facing his failures honestly.

A loving teacher will help a child or young person to examine his reasons for doing something, and to reflect upon the results of his action for others and for himself.

An example of this is to be seen in a certain preschool department. Denise arrived in a storm of tears. Her mother half-pushed her into the room, saying, "That is the stubbornest child I know. She cried all the way over here to bring her crayons. I finally gave in, but it was against my better judgment." Then to Denise:

"I suppose now you'll think you can run the whole house. I hope your father doesn't find out about this—he'll beat me."

The mother left, and Denise, tears streaming down her face, crayons clutched in her hand, walked slowly to the block corner where Cary was building an elaborate tower. She watched for a moment, then kicked the tower over.

How could her teacher treat Denise so as to help her understand the meaning of love? Standing her in a corner would not help. On the other hand, Cary, who was innocent, had been wronged by her actions.

The teacher knelt beside Denise and put her arm gently but firmly around her. "I understand that you feel bad, Denise (an effort to see the world as Denise sees it at the moment), and it's all right to feel bad. Everybody feels bad now and then; but even if you feel bad, you can't tear down what someone else has done (to help her see the results of her behavior for someone else). Cary worked a long time on that tower and it will take a lot of work to fix it again (to interpret how the injured person feels). I am going to help him fix it, and you can help me. Together we can help him build it again (to help her participate in breaching the separation, in repairing the damage)." After they had worked for a while, the teacher took Denise on her lap and held her close. Denise slowly relaxed her tense muscles and smiled companionably at her teacher.

Teaching so as to enact love involves communication and listening—a two-way process. The one-way street of "teacher talks, children listen" is not enough. The teacher must listen in order to know what the children or young people need most deeply, and must help them learn to listen to each other. ("Harry, Nancy has been wanting to say something for quite a while." "Sarah, I don't believe Ann finished what she was saying a while ago. Would you let her say it again?" "Jim has said something awfully important—can you figure out why it is important?") Slowing the pace of participation so that reticent children can participate, interpreting the contributions of certain children so that all can understand them, helping each to feel that his contribution is needed and worthwhile—these are simple but important ways of helping a group learn to communicate and listen.

The teacher will know the names of all the students, for to be called by one's correct name is important to everyone and designates him as unique. However, the teacher will want to know more than names, and will devise ways in which a warm acquaintance between him and the pupils and between the pupils themselves may develop. He may invite small groups to his home for making fudge, roasting marshmallows in the fireplace, cooking a meal together outdoors, or simply (in the case of older children or young people) having a "bull session." He may plan class outings, so that he can know the members informally and listen for their uninhibited enthusiasms and "gripes." He may hold extra work sessions for special activities. Any means by which the wall of separation can be broken down so that members of the class may feel free with one another and with him becomes a "teaching procedure."

The Christian church has the peculiar opportunity to enact in its life what it teaches. A child may have the discussion and stories in his group reinforced by experiences of valuing others and of being valued, of loving and being loved, of trusting and being trusted, and of participating in a supporting fellowship. This is what we mean when we say that children and young people need to belong to a group that demonstrates in its life the distinctive quality of Christian living.

The characteristics mentioned do not exhaust the meaning of being a Christian. Worship and renewal, experiences of the holy and mysterious, and redemptive suffering have not been dealt with. Those mentioned are illustrative and may provoke further exploration of the relation between the Christian life and the living in a class group.

PROCEDURES CONSISTENT WITH
CHRISTIAN LIFE

1. Each Person Becomes Involved

Learning will not become significant in the lives of students unless they want to learn. They can be helped to learn if they are encouraged to feel free to express their differences from authorities, whether teachers or texts.[3]

The aim in teaching is to encourage the learner to formulate for himself the *meaning* of what he is studying and to develop a personal point of view regarding it. Each halting attempt on the part of a student to construct a point of view is encouraged. The development of a personal understanding of life, rather than the imitation of another's views, is important.

A senior-high student, having taken part in a year-long discussion of the life of Jesus, wrote the following on his evaluation at the end of the course:

> The first night was really upsetting to me. The teacher kept asking "Why?" every time I made a statement about Jesus. Before that, I had accepted everything I was taught. That night I realized I didn't know why, but the questioning made me want to know more. The most amazing thing was that what I said and thought mattered. Nobody made fun of what I said, or tried to correct it. I got the feeling that my ideas were worth something; and feeling that way I have been able to express ideas that before I had never tried to express. I believe that the combination of being pushed to think critically and of feeling free to express myself helped me to grow up in my Christian faith.

In contrast, a sixth-grade teacher told her superintendent, "I am shocked every Sunday by the irreverence of my class toward

[3] Nathaniel F. Cantor, *Dynamics of Learning* (Buffalo: Foster and Stewart Publishing Corporation, 1956), p. xiv.

the Bible. They keep asking questions and wondering if it means what it says. I told them last Sunday they were disputing God. They just don't have enough background to ask questions and criticize the Bible, and I, for one, am not going to allow it. They are here to learn about the Bible, not to question it, and I will not preside over the dismemberment of the Bible by a group of sixth-graders!"

This teacher could not have been farther from preserving the spirit of the Bible. Scholars are continually asking questions about the Bible and searching for the truth. The very structure of life as God created it insists on quest and change.

This does not imply that each generation will write its own Bible, but that it must go through the tortuous process of finding the meaning of the Bible in the light of its own situation. One of the most significant things that Jesus did was to reformulate for his day the heritage of Judaism. He questioned religious practices of the day, not to destroy or displace them, but to find new ways in which they could contribute to the true worship of God.

Jesus' method was seldom that of lecturing, never that of requiring repetition or verbal duplication of his "teachings." He demanded wholehearted participation of his learners, without which they could not understand his message. In revisiting Nazareth, he found a detachment and skepticism on the part of the people that made it impossible for him to reach them: "And he did not do many mighty works there, because of their unbelief." (Matt. 13:58)

Jesus said, "Your faith has made you well" (Luke 18:42), placing the emphasis on the active involvement of the spirit of the person seeking help.

His teaching demanded involvement in another way: a willingness to struggle with his words until the meaning was clear. His teaching was often by figure of speech or by stories which the disciples later asked him to explain. The bystander might hear the story, but the meaning was reserved for those who were willing to wrestle with it.

The teacher's major concern is not with memorization or intellectual acceptance of the faith, but with helping students to struggle seriously with its meaning. A junior-high girl, who had recently moved to a new town, came home from church school the first Sunday with shining eyes, saying, "I'm going there every week. Boy! That teacher really made me think."

When her mother pressed her for details, she said, "Whenever I said anything, she seemed to think it was important; then she made us all look at what I said to see what it meant. She did the same with the Bible. She asked questions that made us *think* about what it meant."

Rather than disapprove or stifle critical thinking, this teacher encouraged it. She did this by becoming a questioner—without being an opponent or a threatener. Her students did not try to guess the answer that would please her, for they knew that thinking for themselves would please her most.

Questions that best stimulate thinking are those that call for more than a "yes" or "no" answer or a recitation of known facts—that require a personal reaction. Questions such as the following are illustrative: Could you put it in other words? What would be an example? Would this be an example? Is this what you are saying? What do you mean by —————? How do you know? What are the weaknesses of the idea? If that is true, would this be true? Would you tell us a little more? What is the evidence? Is that conclusion justified on the basis of the evidence?[4]

The teacher whose aim is to involve each student in a personal quest acts as a resource rather than an authority. He tries to help students develop their own point of view. He bears in mind Jesus' reminder, "There is none save God who is good," and points always beyond his own finite understanding to the wisdom

[4] Robert H. Ennis, "Critical Thinking: More on its Motivation," *Progressive Education*, May 1956, p. 76.

and goodness of God. He welcomes questioning and probing by his students, even when his own ideas are challenged. He is prepared for the impatience of students who want to be relieved of the painful task of personal searching and who say, "Tell us what you think. You know the answers." He does not withhold his own point of view, nor the views of others, but always attempts to use them to keep open, rather than to stop, thoughtful searching. The pupils begin to see that they, as well as the teacher, are responsible for their own learning; that it matters what they think; and that what they think has bearing on the direction which the class takes.

2. The Group Carries Responsibility

William Kilpatrick says,

Granted . . . reasonably sympathetic and wise management on the part of teachers, it is possible to get any typical group of children or youth very happily at work along these lines:
1. choosing ever better projects and activities and experiences to undertake
2. planning how to manage and apportioning the work among all the participants
3. executing the plans, changing these if developments so direct; and
4. judging the results, not with intent to apportion praise or blame or even just credit, but to learn how to carry on such an experience better next time.[5]

Part of the teacher's responsibility is to help the group learn how to choose and plan its own activities. He will provide many alternatives, but the group makes the final decision. A junior teacher, in a letter to her former director of religious education, commented on the difference made in her class by the attempt to follow the four steps outlined above:

[5] William Heard Kilpatrick, *Philosophy of Education* (New York: The Macmillan Company, 1951), p. 260.

It is hard for me to describe what has changed. There is a difference in the whole atmosphere of the class. No longer is it all dependent on me. Because the children decided three weeks ago to invite a special resource person and to make a play, they come to class with purposefulness. They are not fiddling around before class starts, but are ready to start early. I have a different feeling about it, too—there is more unity, and I have less of a Sunday-to-Sunday feeling. I have been amazed at their excitement about being on a committee, and at how well they work. I have to watch out that they are not over-critical of slackers. Some of the youngsters have individual projects. The most rewarding thing is their response to the idea of evaluating the work. Sometimes they are too harsh and I have to step in, but at least I don't get the feeling that I have to crack the whip like I did when I was planning everything myself. I have lots more to learn about teaching in this way, but these are my beginning enthusiasms.

As children and young people learn to work on committees, in individual projects, and on activities planned and evaluated by the group, they become self-motivating. The teacher ceases to be the master and becomes the catalytic agent—a role no less demanding but more satisfying. The teacher is no longer a disciplinarian, but a friend to each pupil. He no longer needs to guard his role as controller, for all have a part in controlling.

There is a close relation between class morale or discipline and responsible group planning, as is indicated in the above letter. At their first session, a group not only will make plans for activities, projects, and committee work, but will draw up some rules for fruitful living together. If the rules are "tested" or violated by members of the group, the teacher need not be reproachful, but can indicate, "This is the way we decided it has to be for us to live together. Let's get on with it, then." The teacher also will involve the group in deciding when the rules have been violated, so that at each step of the group life the members learn voluntary assumption of responsibility for their own behavior, rather than mere obedience to outside commands or rules.

Irresponsible and lackadaisical students need particular attention. Public chastisement and punishment seldom make them more responsible participants. A private weekday conversation may help uncover reasons why the students have acted as they have and clues to how they can once again become participants in the group. "I've been wondering, John, what has gone wrong with our class for you. You have good ideas and we need you, but recently we haven't been in the same ball park. Can you give me some clues?" The teacher must be ready to take the student's feelings and comments seriously, even if they call for changes in class procedures.

Responsible group life grows out of many things: personal relations between teacher and pupil and between pupil and pupil, in which each feels that he counts and that it matters what he does and thinks; varied, interesting activities, appropriate to the age group, planned and evaluated by the group itself; group climate that encourages individual participation and cooperative action.

Neither the passive acceptance of rules of behavior authoritatively given, nor rebellious refusal to accept any rules, characterize the life of a Christian group. Docility and passivity are no more Christian virtues than are hostility and rebellion. The middle way of responsibly chosen goals and rules, continually evaluated, seems to lead in the direction of responsible Christian living.

3. The Group Must Evaluate and Reflect

Responsible Christian living calls for self-examination. It is through evaluation and reflection that an individual or a group gains insight for improving the quality of living.

A group may evaluate through examination of the progress made toward goals it has set. It may reflect upon the quality of its life: How well are the members participating? Are the pro-

cedures orderly? Do members carry responsibility and coop-
erate? An individual member may discuss with the teacher the
results of his participation.

Evaluation may take place weekly, as part of the class session,
or occasionally, as at the end of a unit of study or activity or
when a crisis arises. Some classes, especially of older children and
young people, periodically use a written sheet on which members
indicate anonymously their feelings about the class. Other classes
do the same thing verbally, each person stating his feeling about
present or past sessions. In discovering that some members are
bored or feel on the fringe, each member is made more sensitive
to the feelings of others.

Never is evaluation one-sided, with the teacher saying how she
feels about the group. The emphasis is on: "How are *we* doing?
How can we do this better?"

One public school kindergarten teacher daily helps children
learn the skills of reflection and evaluation. The evaluation is not
always for the purpose of correcting mistakes or improving group
work. Successes and good times are reflected upon, with a view
to understanding how and why things happened as they did, and
what the class can do to insure an equally good experience the
next time.

Children in that group soon learn that vague generalizations
("We just didn't get along very good!") are met with a demand
for thinking and analysis ("Why was that so? What could we do
differently? What would be a better idea?"). Irresponsible attempts to shift the blame ("Johnny was a bad boy.") are met with
insistence on honest self-analysis ("Was Johnny the only reason
for our bad day? What happened that made Johnny act the way
he did? What do you think we could do about it?").

Children and young people who are allowed—indeed, urged—
to express their own reactions and feelings about what is happening to them begin to feel responsible for shaping what happens to them. They can tell whether a teacher is willing to have

the group procedures changed in order to take seriously the suggestions made. They can also tell whether a teacher genuinely cares how they feel about themselves and the group. They begin to see how their life is affected by their responsible or irresponsible behavior, attitudes, and feelings.

A class need not be a conglomeration of children or young people which a teacher must keep quiet in order to teach. It is a laboratory, a workshop, a proving ground in which the members may learn in a double way what it means to be Christian. Their life together in the group may become a most important means for discovering the meaning of love, forgiveness, understanding, responsibility, failure, reflection, concern, freedom, self-revelation, humility. Insofar as the ways of living together in a group are in the spirit of the verbal teaching, the members have a "double-learning" opportunity.

III

The Two Languages
of Teaching

The teaching language of the Christian fellowship "is the language of relations, the language of life lived together. Later, after children have participated somewhat in the life of the Christian fellowship and have come to possess its meanings for them, they will hear, with growing understanding, the fellowship's words about its faith. Then the teaching may continue, both by the language of relations and the language of words, each language assisting and complementing the other."[1]

The "language of relations"—two-way, person-to-person relations—may well be the most effective means for teaching or learning Christianity. The Hebrew-Christian faith affirms that God is known in the events of everyday life and in the life of nations. It is in human relations, therefore, that God reveals himself; indeed, his decisive Word to mankind came in the form of a person. We know God, according to Christianity, not so much as the ordainer of ideas, principles, and rules as a Reality experienced in personal life.

[1] Reuel L. Howe, "Children Can Find Christian Fellowship," *International Journal of Religious Education*, March 1959, p. 47.

In a recent survey, it was found that few adults remember more than one or two of their childhood teachers. One woman who remembered a certain teacher was questioned about the reason for remembering. She looked at the floor for a while then answered in two words, "She cared."

Sometimes in our zeal for teaching a lesson, we neglect the caring. There is important information that children and young people need to acquire in becoming acquainted with the Christian way of life. Yet our teaching needs to be carried on with the language of relations as well as the language of words. The classroom must be a place where the Christian good news is enacted as well as talked about. Knowing the principles of Christianity, or being able to repeat its teachings, does not guarantee an ability to live as a Christian any more than knowing the rules of tennis insures an ability to play the game. It is in the relations of friend and friend, parent and child, teacher and pupil, friend and foe, that one begins to practice the Christian life.

A child or young person learns from the way he is treated how to treat others. He learns this in the home, the school, the church, and the community. The experiences which a child or youth has may undergird his Christian life or may negate it.

> The parent—who is gentle with the family pets; who is tender with clumsiness; who shows concern for the scratches and bruises of the youngster; who helps out a sick neighbor—is building an atmosphere in which young people can grow into a healthy tenderness. . . . The sense of moral values cannot be wedged into a child by admonition. It has to come as the fine flowering of his experience.[2]

A young person may learn the verbal petition, "Forgive us our debts as we forgive our debtors," while learning in his associa-

[2] Reprinted by permission of the Association for Childhood Education International, 3615 Wisconsin Avenue, N.W., Washington 16, D.C. "Building Sound Personality," by Harry and Bonaro Overstreet. From *Childhood Education,* April 1956, Vol. 32, No. 8, pp. 358 and 359.

tions with people that forgiveness is hard-bought, that mistakes are often irreparable in the eyes of adults, that grudges are carried overlong because no one is willing to admit that he is wrong.

A child may learn with his lips that "Honesty is the best policy," but observe that, in order to be in favor with the teacher, he must say he has read the Bible every day whether he has or not.

He may learn "to give and not to count the cost," while at the same time he finds that his parents and teachers are not interested in the gifts he offers them: crude drawings, feathers, rocks, or sticks discovered by the path. He sees his treasures, given to adults he cares for, laid aside while conversation is continued, smiled at patronizingly, or ignored.

It is in the intimacy of associations with others that life is changed—for better or for worse. If the association is one of mutual respect, the conditions for learning are present.

Martin Buber, the great Jewish philosopher, has pointed to the relationship of person with person as the arena for significant learning and for discovering God's activity. He emphasizes that there must be a dialogue between the teacher and the learner, a meeting of two real selves (as distinguished from the meeting of a self and a thing, or of a thing and a thing).

Although the word *dialogue* implies two-sidedness, our relations in the classroom often tend to be in monologues or dual monologues. This may be a peculiar pitfall of the teaching-learning association, because of the difference in age and experience of teacher and pupils. There seem to be two safeguards which may help us to have true communication and therefore an occasion through which the eternal Thou can speak. One of these safeguards is the recognition of the distinctiveness of the pupil as a unique individual; the other is the recognition of the distinctiveness of the teacher as a unique individual. Martin Buber says that a real meeting of two selves is possible only insofar as the "otherness" of each is observed and acted upon.[3] This involves a recognition that neither person is putty to be molded by the other nor a mirror of the other's desires and wishes, but a distinctive person, different from any other person, adult or child.

The idea that a teacher must recognize the otherness or distinctiveness of the pupil may seem a bit puzzling, for unity, or identity, between teacher and pupil also is needed. But only as a teacher respects the otherness of each pupil can he build with his students the relations in which Christian teaching and learning can take place.

Carl R. Rogers, who has validated in clinical practice the importance of person-to-person associations, says,

> The degree to which I can create relationships which facilitate the growth of others as separate persons is a measure of the growth I have achieved in myself. In some respects this is a disturbing thought, but it is also a promising or challenging one. It would indicate that if I am interested in creating helping relationships I have a fascinating life-time job ahead of me, stretching and developing my potentials in the direction of growth. . . .[4]

The importance of recognizing the distinctiveness of the pupil is emphasized by the Hebrew-Christian assertion that each person is a child of God, worthful in and for himself. He must not, therefore, be manipulated or used.

The teacher's appreciation of the otherness of the learner changes their relation to each other from that of a superior with an inferior to one between two creatures of God the Father. Although the teacher knows more than the student, is older, more experienced, and wiser, he sees the learner as a center of under-

[3] Martin Buber, "The Teacher and Teaching," a collection of writings collated by Ross Snyder, Chicago Theological Seminary; abridged from *Between Man and Man*, by Martin Buber (Boston: Beacon Press, 1955).

[4] Carl R. Rogers, "The Characteristics of a Helping Relationship," *Personnel and Guidance Journal*, Vol. 37, Sept. 1958, pp. 6-16.

standing, purposing, energy, and perception. Each student is a unique creation of God, to whom he responds personally, not as a member of a faceless group.

Without respect for the distinctiveness of the learner, teaching can easily drift into disregard of the learner's part in determining the values by which he shall live.

Stand Within the Student's World

To appreciate the distinctiveness of each of his students, a teacher must become skilled in at least two ways: seeing things from the student's perspective, and learning to understand and accept his feelings.

The teacher will try to get inside his student's world of thinking, perceiving, and understanding. This is done, not in an effort to control, but in order to know deeply what the other person is like and to know how to communicate with him.

One result of standing within the world of the student is a serious regard for his efforts to put together his many experiences into a rational whole. Often, in piecing together what he knows about the world, a child comes up with ideas that seem funny to an adult, but the sensitive teacher will not laugh unless the child is laughing. The limited time-sense of young children makes it difficult for them to understand much of the church's teaching about things that happened many years ago. A first-grade child, whose father was born in 1918, asked her mother, "Did Jesus live about the time of the first World War?" She knew that her father had been born during the war, which was a long time ago. She also knew that Jesus lived long ago. The mother took a piece of string and measured off an inch to represent the time since 1918. Then she measured off over a yard, and told the child that Jesus had lived longer ago than the time represented by the string. She added that the child was correct, however, in thinking that Jesus and Daddy had something to do with each other, for although

Jesus lived many years ago his spirit is still with us today. By showing respect for the child's attempt to put together what she knew, the mother was able to give her new insight.

A kindergartner had been to a museum where there was a display of Egyptian relics. She was fascinated by the mummy cases. Later in the week she said, "Mommy, how do poor mothers have babies?" "What do you mean?" her mother asked before jumping into an explanation of reproduction. "I mean, because they don't have doctors and medicine. Don't they die?" "Yes, sometimes they do die, especially in parts of the world where people are very poor." "When the mothers die, do they put them in the Mommy cases we saw at the museum?" Laughing would have blocked further venturing, but dealing seriously with her question enabled the child to continue piecing together her world—a process that she must carry on throughout life if life is to make sense.

In trying to see things as children and young people see them, a teacher will encourage the students to express their impressions of things as they see them. When the impressions are inaccurate or ludicrous, he will attempt gently to help the persons to secure more adequate information so that they can reformulate their ideas. His primary concern will be to keep in tune with the way his students see things.

To see things as the learner sees them is a demanding and continuing task for the teacher, parent, or anyone concerned with helping persons grow. The teacher must help the students to see life as it really is, without depreciating their partial or confused attempts to understand. The teacher must assist in the search for what is true without taking over what each person must do for himself. Children and young people must evaluate and reshape ideas that are erroneous, hazy, or half-true. The teacher can encourage accurate thinking without labeling ideas as wrong. Children and young people feel free to formulate ideas of their own if they can be sure that their teacher will not ridicule them or label them "wrong."

A high school teacher who has made an attempt over several years to see things as teen-agers see them had an interesting experience. She writes,

> I was searching for a way to make the Bible something more than a relic from the past for teen-agers. They talked politely about Jesus' teachings, but in occasional flashes of honesty they said it just didn't connect up with their own living. So, one night, I had the irreverent (perhaps) idea of having them translate the Bible into their own language. One boy "translated" the story of the rich man and his barns. Although unorthodox, I submit that this gets at the heart of that parable (Luke 12:16-22).
>
>> A kid who had lots of money said to himself, "What will I do because I don't have any place to keep my Cadillac? I will tear down my garages and build bigger ones. Then I will have room for my convertible and MG too. And then I'll say, 'Kid, you've got it made! Take it easy! Live it up!'"
>> But God said, "You're a fool. Tonight you die, and now what will happen to your cars? Money isn't everything."
>> So, don't worry so much about things like convertibles, steaks, and cashmeres.

In learning to see things as the pupil sees them, a teacher needs to develop the ability to accept and deal with feelings that do not coincide with his own. An example of this is seen in the way two teachers dealt with the same situation, as follows:

CHILD: "I hate Sunday school. I don't like to come to church."
TEACHER: "You must not say that! This is the house of God."
CHILD: "I still don't like to come."
TEACHER: "Why, of course, you do. You know that verse we say every Sunday: 'I was glad when they said unto me, Let us go into the house of the Lord.'"

This teacher refused to recognize the feelings of the child, and insisted that he pretend he did not feel negative about coming to church.

Another teacher responded to the negative feelings this way:

CHILD: "I hate Sunday school. I don't like to come to church."

TEACHER: "Would you like to tell me more about how you feel?"

In the conversation that followed, the second teacher found out that the child disliked intensely doing things with his hands—drawing, clay modeling, painting. He had a strong feeling that he was no good at any of these things. Most of the class activities had called for the use of his hands, and he felt more and more bitter. This teacher, by listening to what the child had to say, was able to change the class situation so that he again became an interested participant.

Listening and accepting feelings does not imply approval or disapproval of them. No judgment of any kind is involved. The teacher attempts to see things as the child sees them, so that he can help him understand his feelings and do something constructive about them.

Most adults are not accustomed to expressing, or having children and young people express, feelings of hostility, fear, or anger. It is difficult, therefore, for them to understand that anything constructive can happen by accepting a child's or young person's negative feelings. They think that it will give the student the impression that what he says is approved and will make him feel it more strongly after the conversation. In most cases, precisely the opposite is true. The power of a negative feeling is often diminished when it is shared with someone. It no longer seems so frightening or compelling. This is especially true if the person with whom it is shared tries to see from the perspective of the person speaking before attempting to help.

Children and young people sometimes have misconceptions which they are afraid to reveal to adults. For example, a child who is told that God will punish him if he is naughty or thinks bad thoughts may think accidents or misfortune are God's punishment. A high school junior said to his church youth counselor, "God punishes badness, doesn't he? Then, if a person's mother dies, that is a punishment for his badness, isn't it?" After hours of conversation, the counselor discovered that once in his childhood the boy had expressed negative feelings about his mother, and someone had told him God would punish him for being such a bad boy. Shortly thereafter his mother died, and he had felt personally responsible, certain that his words had produced his mother's death. In conversation with his counselor he had faced this long-held fear for the first time. Although it will be a long time, if ever, before all the effects of this fear are dissipated, talking about it with an understanding person seemed to lessen the load.

The reassurance that all people have bad feelings of one sort or another is often helpful. An understanding listener often frees a person to begin doing something about what he fears or hates.

Katherine Read, writing to nursery school teachers, says,

> We've been taught so often that we must be "good" that we are afraid to recognize the negative feelings that exist in us. They go unrecognized and interfere with our thinking more than they would if we had accepted them. As adults we can afford to look at them squarely because we have the capacity for self-control. . . . It is not for us to say whether people ought or ought not to feel and act as they do. We make very little progress when we blame or praise them or ourselves for the way they or we feel and act. We make progress when we try to understand why we act as we do. Getting angry or discouraged with ourselves or anyone else is unprofitable. It is usually tremendously profitable to recognize that we can do something to change our ways of feeling and acting if we choose.[5]

[5] Katherine Haskill Read, *The Nursery School* (Philadelphia: W. B. Saunders Company, 1955), pp. 14 and 15.

As a teacher grows in ability to look at things from the child's or young person's vantage point and to accept his feelings, he will understand why he must not have a person-thing attitude toward his students. In a person-thing relation with the student, a teacher uses him to achieve some purpose. The Christmas and Children's Day programs in some churches illustrate the way in which children are often used as things. To show the parents and the church that they have learned something, children are arranged in front of the congregation and each "says" something. What he says is not what he would say if he were free to choose, nor is it usually anything that adds depth to his personal living. It is intended to show off the children, to reassure the adults that children are learning something.

Some teaching procedures create a person-thing relation. The use of handwork with an emphasis on the product rather than on creation and expression is an example. The teacher wants children to know that God has planned for growth and that flowers are an example of this plan; so she cuts out patterns of flowers, leaves, and pots, and the children paste them according to a model which the teacher provides. Except for exercise in seeing different shapes, practice in copying, and the fun of working with paste, there is little learning. It is doubtful that any of the learning the teacher had in mind is achieved. The child's abilities are used to copy something the teacher planned, rather than to express something he helped to conceive.

Another class is quiet and orderly. The teacher has formulated rules—no talking without raising one's hand; no moving from one's assigned seat; speaking allowed only when recognized. The calm exterior of the class is deceptive, for underneath are myriad individual feelings, reactions, concerns, fears, and hopes. These may not be expressed unless they happen to fall within the rules. In an effort to achieve order, the teacher has stultified the pupils, and smothered the possibility of communication through the language of relations.

This does not imply that there should be no rules. Fruitful

group life can take place only within boundaries which allow for both order and freedom. But children, even small ones, are able to help formulate the boundaries. They can discuss what has been happening in the group ("How do you feel our day went?") and make proposals for ways of changing it ("Do you think of ways we could have a better day next time?"). The individual member is no longer a tool, but a fashioner. He is not a thing which is used, but a person whose ideas are utilized for the good of all.

The Teacher's Uniqueness Also Must Be Respected

In the dialogue between persons, if one is thought to be inferior to the other, there will be exploitation and domination—and this is true whether the dominated one be the child or the teacher. In the dialogue there must be intercommunication between two real selves. Insofar as the teacher is free to be himself (alive, vital, unique) rather than a stereotype of what a teacher should be (dignified, all-knowing, stern, punishing), he can enter into a creative dialogue with students. In living face to face with persons who are free to be themselves without pretense, children and young people catch the vitality of living religiously.

Some teachers and parents, having heard that children must be respected, proceed to disrespect themselves, reducing themselves to slaves of the students. One cannot help another to become a person if he himself is a nonentity. The teacher as well as the pupil must search constantly for insight and courage to understand the kind of person he is and the kind he wants to become. He must be free to express his ideas, insights, and feelings, at the same time making sure that each pupil has the opportunity to do the same.

A Teacher Must Be Open-Minded in His Conviction

The teacher who seeks to grow in ability to enter into a two-way communication with children or young people must live with open-minded conviction about Christianity. "Open-minded conviction" seems a contradiction in terms, yet it is the state in which Christians must live. If we are convinced of the good news of Christianity, we must live with conviction that it makes sense for all of life. Every person lives on the basis of some interpretation of what is most real for him. Yet this interpretation must be freshened constantly by questions—yes, by doubts—and be open to new revelation of truth which might break forth in any experience. We do not possess the final formulation of God's truth to give to children and young people. But we have that by which we are willing to live, praying that we may be able to recognize new insights. Conviction and teachableness, surety and receptivity, are important characteristics of the teacher who hopes to carry on a helpful dialogue with his students.

Related is the courage to be creative—to share with God in his ongoing creative action. Made in the image of the Creator, we find our deepest satisfaction when we are creating—a painting, a cake, a relationship, a new understanding, a new patio. Each of us finds an inner harmony when he is able to bring into being something that has form and purpose where previously there was nothing; to watch something develop from chaotic formlessness to design due to his efforts. Creation involves the willingness to venture into ways where one has never been before. One cannot, therefore, be a creative teacher and say, "But I can't try that—I've never done it." The price paid for creativity is sometimes the willingness to abandon familiar teaching procedures in order that something new may be created.

If one is dealing with a group of students in the same way he himself was treated as a youngster, it is doubtful whether much creative teaching is happening. A part of being a creative teacher is the willingness and maturity to examine not only one's teaching procedures but one's feelings and reactions to the group. Honest and objective self-evaluation is difficult but not impossible.

TEACHER TO SELF: Why does Stan always do such bothersome things?

SELF: Is it that he does bothersome things, or that you are easily bothered?

TEACHER: Any child who gets himself covered to the elbow every time he is near paint is certainly a nuisance.

SELF: Does the fact that you were never allowed to "mess" in paint have anything to do with your reaction?

TEACHER: How silly! What does that have to do with it?

SELF: Just this, Stan doesn't disturb the class or hold up the work, does he? No, he just gets messy. And he always cleans the paint off himself, which doesn't take your time or that of the class. Let's face it, you just don't feel it's quite right for children to get messy in class. And why not? Because you don't feel comfortable when they do. Isn't that the reason basically that Diane appeals to you so much—she is neat and clean and careful, just the way you were taught proper children should be?

TEACHER: You're right. Why didn't I see that before now?

A teacher who had participated in discussions of the building of person-to-person relations in teaching said, puzzled, "I know that we have something in this matter of loving relationships, but aren't we a bit presumptuous in assuming that God is working through us?"

This question ought to prod us into continual self-examination and prayer. We must never make an easy identification of God's way of working with ours. "His ways are not our ways." Yet we must be open to all means by which his spirit may speak to us and through us. ". . . if God has loved us so, we ought to love one another. No one has ever seen God; yet if we love one another, God keeps in union with us. . . ."[6]

[6] I John 4:11, *The New Testament—An American Translation,* by Edgar J. Goodspeed (Chicago: The University of Chicago Press).

PART TWO

PROCEDURES
FOR VARIOUS
AGE GROUPS

THE FIRST THREE CHAPTERS HAVE FOCUSED
attention on the importance of a biblical perspective in teaching, combined with a concern to
enact in the life of the group what it is to be
Christian. Emphasis has been placed on the necessity for the involvement of each student in
the continual search for life's meanings and in
the development of his own Christian outlook.

In the next seven chapters these concerns are
not left behind, but are seen as coming out of the
experience of groups and their leaders who have
had enough imagination to attempt new ways
of learning together. Attention is given to specific
teaching-learning procedures and the ways in
which they can foster the discovery of what it
means to be related to God.

It is interesting to see how the principles discussed in the preceding chapters actually work
out as teachers and their groups follow them in
building their life together. Each of the next
seven chapters shows what can happen as a

group uses a variety of related learning ventures to experience the Christian faith as well as to hear about it. A variety of teaching procedures is used, not because variety in itself is good, but because several procedures used in relation to each other can provide a deep and rich learning experience.

Chapter IV deals somewhat in general with the use of many related procedures, but is directed toward lower junior and older children. Each of the next six chapters shows how a variety of learning procedures can be used with a specific age group, beginning with preschool and continuing to senior high school. Some groups will find it possible and desirable to use as many procedures as are described in a chapter. Others may find it necessary to select fewer. In each case, procedures that serve the purpose of a class best should be used. Detailed suggestions concerning many procedures will be found in Chapters XI to XVII.

IV

Use Clusters of
Experiences

The crucial question which a teacher faces in sharing the Christian faith with children or young people is: "How can I help this faith to 'come alive' for the members of this group? How can it become a part of them?"

It is generally true that a depth of appreciation and understanding comes as one sees something from various angles. One can, for instance, appreciate the beauty of a lake by looking at a picture of it. But when one walks beside it in the sunlight, splashes in it, rides on it in a boat, looks at it from the top of a dune, watches a storm approaching across it, listens to its roars and whispers, and describes its moods to a friend, his appreciation of the lake is greatly increased. The use of several teaching procedures that provide a cluster of related experiences brings a reality and depth to learning otherwise not likely to be achieved.

The spirit which Protestant religious education hopes to encourage in its children and youth is that of exploration or inquiry rather than passive receptivity. This spirit is undeveloped if minds and imaginations are always forced along the same path.

It is stimulated as persons are exposed to a rich variety of learning experiences. Not until the student has the "Aha!" experience can what is taught begin to operate from within.

Many teachers have discovered one exciting teaching procedure; others have found two or three. The real challenge is for teachers to refuse to be content with using one or two approaches, and to seek new ways of making learning a living process.

Variety in teaching procedures does not mean a hodgepodge of novel approaches—a shower of miscellaneous techniques piled one upon the other. It involves a many-faceted, imaginative approach with an inner consistency. The procedures support one another, the parts complementing each other to make a whole experience. They are integrally related to each other, flowing out of what has gone before, anticipating what is to come.

Without a relatedness between the various activities carried on within a group, the learning ventures may actually interfere with each other. Isolated experiences, no matter how varied or interesting, can never have the impact of a series or cluster of experiences that are integrally related. There is no place for "busy work" in any form.

THE TEACHER AS A PERSON IS PRIMARY

No set of teaching procedures will be effective unless there are understanding and trust between the teacher and his students. The kind of person one *is* is primary—even more basic than the kinds of teaching procedures one uses, for a contagious Christian faith is transmitted directly from person to person. To be sure, many facts about the Christian faith are communicated by the teacher, but so are many intangibles: understanding, forgiveness, concern. The teacher shares his personhood as well as his beliefs. His commitment to his students and to the Christian faith shines through any method he may use.

A child's or young person's sense of his individual worth is enhanced in this kind of association and is destroyed by mistrust, scolding, and misunderstanding. To love a member of the group is to show concern for him, to attempt to understand why he is as he is, and to accept him. The experience of being loved, prized, and accepted is basic in Christian nurture. Without it, verbal teaching about God's love or man's is likely to miss the mark.

The sense of worthfulness is enhanced by trust between the child or young person and an understanding and mature adult. It is enlarged through participation in a group in which faith in one's worthfulness is lived out—where one is allowed to assume responsibility, make decisions, plan ahead, and evaluate. Relations of this kind not only enhance the student's sense of worth, but develop group morale and create a climate in which learning is likely to be lasting.

Children achieve self-confidence, ability in self-direction, and a sense of worth as the teacher is able to work in cooperation with them rather than wielding power over them, to trust them with responsibility rather than fearing their immaturity, to let them make choices instead of protecting them from failure. Given such relations between group and teacher, the imaginative use of related teaching procedures has a great deal to do with the quality of teaching and learning.

ROOM AND WORSHIP AFFECT LEARNING

The room in which the group meets and the worship in which it engages can have an influence on learning. The room must speak of interesting things—must open new vistas and intrigue members of the group into further exploration. It must be allowed to reflect the interests of the persons who use it: their plans will be listed, their creations displayed, their committees and interest groups posted. Pictures, models, curios, maps, charts, questions on the blackboard, books, posters—all play their part in helping the room teach. Even if the "room" is a corner of a large room or a church pew, it can still belong uniquely to the group that meets there, stimulating interest and inviting new inquiry each week. Imagination on the part of the teacher can help make any meeting area a teaching area.

Richness can be added to learning by experiences of worship. Worship should be related to the teaching, and often arises out of the experience of learning. The moments of awe, of discovery, of wonder, when a child stands breathless before something new or beautiful, for example, are times of real worship. Sometimes the sensitive teacher will allow a child to stand in wonder without interpretation; at other times he may lead the child to find an appropriate hymn or poem, to offer a silent prayer of thanksgiving, or to meditate.

Varied Approaches to the 23rd Psalm

Using the 23rd Psalm as a unit of study, let us look more closely at the use of related teaching procedures to help a group of children have a deep and penetrating experience of the Psalm.

The following list taken from a teacher's notebook suggests some of the possibilities. No attempt is made to list these according to age levels, but they are appropriate for use with children of lower junior age (third and fourth grades) and older. These or other activities would be used when the study of the Psalm is developed into a full unit of the curriculum over a period of several sessions.

1. *Look at pictures of sheep, shepherds, and pastoral scenes.* The "still waters," "green pastures," and shepherd life become more real as the children see pictures of them. *National Geographic Magazine* frequently has pictures that can be used. The December 1926 issue contains an article, "Among the Bethlehem Shepherds," with pictures illustrating the 23rd Psalm. The December 1957 issue contains an article on "Bringing Old Testament Times to Life." Many public libraries have picture files and also stereoscopic pictures of the Holy Land.

2. *Examine books, models, and curios.* The care of sheep is remote from the experience of most modern children. It is important to provide as many ways as possible of interpreting the experience out of which the Psalm comes. Seeing the Psalm in several versions of the Bible, possibly including one in another language, will add interest. If a shepherd's crook and a staff, a flute, and a shepherd's pipe are available, children will be interested in them and in an explanation of their uses.

3. *Listen to appropriate recorded music.* The feeling tone of the peace, the excitement, the adventure involved in shepherd life can be caught by children as they listen to music such as Beethoven's *Pastoral Symphony,* Handel's "He Shall Lead His Flock," and Bach's "Sheep May Safely Graze." Each might be played once for quiet listening, then a second time while the children finger-paint in motion and color the way the music makes them feel. After this, members of the group may want to talk about the experience.

4. *Read and talk about the Psalm.* With the children in a quiet and reflective mood, possibly with eyes closed, the Psalm is read from a modern version by the teacher. Then the group can talk about the feelings they had—possibly of calm and freedom from fear—in hearing of God's care. This should be in a mood of appreciation rather than analysis.

5. *Compose a choral-reading version of the Psalm.* A choral reading allows all of the group to participate, helping them to become well enough acquainted with the Psalm to use it with feeling in worship. The reading must be thoughtful and well done, not just a routine "saying" it. The group may work out its own arrangement for choral reading, but the following is one possibility:

SOLO: The Lord is my shepherd, I shall not want.
BOYS: He makes me lie down in green pastures.
GIRLS: He leads me beside still waters;
ALL: He restores my soul.

SOLO: He leads me in paths of righteousness for his name's sake.

BOY: Even though I walk through the valley of the shadow of death, I fear no evil; for thou art with me;

BOYS: Thy rod and thy staff, they comfort me.

BOY: Thou preparest a table before me in the presence of my enemies;

GIRL: Thou anointest my head with oil,

SOLO: My cup overflows.

ALL: Surely goodness and mercy shall follow me all the days of my life;

SOLO: And I shall dwell in the house of the Lord for ever.

6. *Make a tape recording of the choral reading.* Making a recording has the values of drill but is much more interesting. While doing the choral reading and recording, most of the members of the group will memorize the Psalm. By making a recording, then listening as it is "played back," weak spots can be picked out to be corrected in the second recording. Parts can be recorded as a rehearsal. This can be repeated until a satisfactory recording is made. If someone is available who plays a flute or pipe, a pastoral melody can be played as background music.

7. *Visit a farmer or have him visit the group.* Field trips give a first-hand experience which no amount of reading can provide. If it is possible for the group to visit a sheep farm and talk with the farmer, it will help to bring the Psalm to life. If this is impossible, perhaps someone who has had experience with sheep can visit the group and describe how sheep are cared for.

Before this happens, the group should make a list of questions which they wish to ask the farmer. "What food do sheep eat?" "How do they act?" "How are they sheared of wool?" "How are they cared for?" Sheep farming is different now from what it was in ancient Palestine. Yet the interview can help the members of the group understand the dependence of the sheep on the shepherd for food, water, shelter, protection, and care in illness.

8. *Discuss what makes a good shepherd.* Out of this first-hand experience, the group can pull together its new understanding and list the findings on newsprint or chalkboard. A leisurely conversation about the trip or interview will help the children to reflect upon what they have discovered so far.

9. *Discuss what is learned about God from this Psalm.* The words and background are familiar enough now so that the meaning underneath begins to appear. The boys and girls can begin to understand that this is not a description of pastoral life, but of God's care. The list previously drawn up of the findings about sheep and shepherds will help them see the way in which God's love is like a good shepherd's care for his flock.

10. *Listen to "Puddin' Head's Discovery"* and other records on how we got our Bible, in the set, "Adventures with the Book"[1] —an exciting and dramatic story of the way the Psalm might have been written. It will help children realize how a shepherd, looking at the rolling hills and the heavens, might have said, "The Lord is my shepherd," or "The heavens declare the glory of God."

11. *Draw a frieze or box movie about the writing of the 23rd Psalm.* Talking and finger painting are, to this point, the only ways in which the members of the group have expressed their reaction to the Psalm. Having heard a dramatic story, it is good for them to express their understanding of it. Perfection of art-work is not so important as the involvement of each person in the process of putting to use what he has heard and talked about. Each child, either at home or in class, draws the section of the movie or frieze that he has chosen; the parts are then pasted together in sequence and placed on the wall for a frieze or fastened onto rollers and inserted in a box (with front cut away) for showing as a "movie roll."

[1] This set of two records (LP, double-faced, 10″) is available from Pilgrim Press, 14 Beacon Street, Boston 8, Mass.

12. *Invite a member of the choir to sing some of the hymns and anthems based on the 23rd Psalm.* Having a member of the choir sing to the group helps the boys and girls feel related to the rest of the church, and also helps them understand that the Psalms are songs or hymns. The list of questions previously compiled can be reviewed again, before and after the singing. If a copy of the *Scottish Psalter* is available, it may be interesting to see a hymnal made up exclusively of Psalms.

13. *Learn some hymns based on Psalms, such as "Old 100th," "Dundee," "Stuttgart."* Having heard some music based on Psalms, the group will learn some of the great hymn tunes and words from Psalm origins. With help they can learn to use the index of authors and sources and the index of composers and tunes in the hymnal. They will enjoy looking for hymns based on Psalms, and discovering which hymn tunes come from *Genevan Psalter, Scottish Psalter,* or *Psalmodia Evangelica.*

14. *Compose a hymn tune for the 23rd Psalm.* This will probably be a new experience. Having listened and sung, the boys and girls now become creators of music themselves. As the leader reads the Psalm a line at a time, the children listen intently, imagining what kind of tune would suit these words. As one is ready, he can hum his tune; then others may hum theirs. When a tune seems especially to fit, it is played on the piano and the group moves on to the next line or phrase. When the tune is completed, the group learns it and uses it in worship. A member of the choir might help the group make its tune, especially if the teacher feels insecure in this kind of effort.

15. *Write a group litany or creed.* Writing and using a litany is a good way of reviewing reflectively what has been learned. A litany is a prayer in responsive form, the leader's words and the group's response making a complete sentence. The following is an example of a litany:

LEADER: Let us give thanks for God's loving care.

For your gentle love for us,

GROUP: *We give you thanks, O God.*
LEADER: For your being with us when it is hard or when we
   are in trouble,
GROUP: *We are glad, O God.*
LEADER: For your being always near to us,
GROUP: *We thank you, God.* Amen.

Writing a creed (a statement of belief) can also help the members of the group to make the Psalm their own with overtones of worship. They can dictate their ideas as the teacher writes them down. An example of a creed is:

> We believe that God cares about us, and that he loves us as a
> good shepherd loves his sheep. We believe that God helps us
> when the way is hard. We believe that God knows what we
> need.

16. *Share the learnings.* Sharing their experience with the Psalm gives children a sense of the importance of their undertaking. The group may want to invite the minister, the parents, or another class to see the finger paintings, mural, or box movie; to listen to the choral reading, hymns, Psalm set to music, and one of the pastoral records; to share in reading the litany or creed; to examine the curios and pictures; to hear any report the group wants to make.

This list of suggestions is by no means complete, but it indicates that any one piece of teaching material is open to the use of many related teaching procedures. Probably no one class would want to use all of them. The use of varied and related explorations makes possible a many-sided imaginative approach to a subject. The procedures need to be related and must support one another. They must build on previous learning, look to future learning, and flow into one another.

Teaching in the way outlined requires time, planning, and imagination, but the effort is well spent if even one child comes to have a deeper appreciation of his dependence on God.

V

Understanding the *Word* Before the Words

(PRESCHOOL)

Teachers of preschool children may have the most important task in the church. Experience at the preschool age is the foundation for all later experience. It is essential, therefore, that the persons working with very young children be sensitive, mature, and dedicated persons with a yearning to understand the nature of a young child and the nature of Reality.

The use of the Bible with small children is perplexing to many preschool teachers. The words, symbols, and stories are often beyond the experience and understanding of young children, for the Bible grew out of adult experience. We cannot assume that a child understands the Bible or appropriates its meaning because he can repeat verses from it or because parts of it have been read to him. Yet even the small child can *experience* the unconditional love and acceptance to which the Bible points. The *meaning* of the biblical drama of creative and redemptive love can be a part of the experience of every preschool child, even when the words of the Bible are not used.

For Andy, aged three, the hearing and repeating of "Forgive us our trespasses as we forgive those who trespass against us" may make little change in his living. But the *meaning* of the words was experienced in something that happened to him in church school.

Andy was helping take care of the turtle in the nursery room. The glass aquarium was large, but children each Sunday carried it to the washroom to change the water. The teacher warned Andy that the aquarium must be carried carefully, for if he walked fast the water might splash out and make the floor slippery. In his eagerness Andy ran, and the water was sloshed onto the floor. Susan, on the way to the book corner, slipped and fell.

Andy looked remorsefully from Susan to the teacher. The teacher put a comforting arm around both children and said, "Andy was very eager to change the turtle's water. Next time he will be more careful. He didn't mean to splash the water where you would slip, Susan. Here, Andy, let's wipe up the water with the sponge we keep for spilled things." Andy began the job tearfully until Susan patted him on the back and said, "It's all right. Andy didn't mean to do it."

Andy learned, through a patient teacher and an understanding child, what it means to be forgiven and received back into loving relations, and Susan reached out in generosity and forgiveness. Each knew in this concrete experience the forgiveness that is at the heart of the Bible message.

The Hebrew-Christian faith has always asserted that history, or life lived each day, is the arena of God's activity, and that it is in our daily living that we come to know God. Young children can experience much that, interpreted by a loving, understanding teacher, becomes the groundwork for a developing awareness of God's activity in their lives. Our purpose in teaching is not to help children repeat words, but to help them have a first-hand experience of what the words mean—to experience the "Word" of the Bible even before the words are understandable.

What does it mean to be a "teacher" of preschool children? Traditionally, a teacher was thought of as one who had a lesson "to get across" to pupils. A person was teaching when he was talking, telling, explaining, or showing. Teaching preschool children—any children, for that matter—is not so much a matter of "getting across a lesson" as it is establishing relationships through which the love of God can be channeled. When teaching is life-to-life, rather than purely verbal, communication is surer and more direct. The teacher looks upon her associations with the child as one of the most important avenues for communicating the love of God.

This "relationship approach" to teaching is based on the understanding that the truths that revolutionize our lives are most often communicated to us through other persons—our parents, our friends, our teachers. We learn more about the nature of love by being caught up in relationships with another person which involve the receiving and giving of love, than we do by hearing a hundred stories and verses with the theme "Beloved, let us love one another."

Roy was a large four-year-old. He seemed self-enclosed from the moment he entered the room. He would stand in the middle of the play area with head down, furtively surveying the room. All attempts to interest him in activities were futile. Suddenly he would lash out at a child who passed by, jerk the hair ribbon from a girl, or push a smaller child out of the rocking-boat.

One of the teachers restrained him from hurting other children, but knew that this was not enough. Something was going on deep inside Roy with which he needed help. The teacher found that he seemed to need to be physically near her, to touch her, and nestle close to her. She asked other teachers to carry her responsibilities and she spent as much time with Roy as he seemed to need. Whenever he made a hostile move toward another child she accepted the fact that he had angry feelings, but explained to him that, although every person sometimes feels angry, he must not hurt other people. All the while she let him be close to her, never letting him drift beyond her concern.

For many weeks, Roy clung to the teacher, following her every-where. Gradually he began to venture into the room for longer and longer periods, occasionally coming back to where the teacher was sitting quietly. It was a red-letter day in the department when he was overheard to say to the girl whose ribbon he had snatched the first day, "Here, Linda. I'll help you build the tower. You don't have enough blocks underneath it to make it stand up straight."

A child was slowly emerging from hostility to concern for others through the patience and love of a teacher. Whether he was able to repeat the verse "Be ye kind" is secondary, for he had known within himself, then transmitted to another, the contagion of loving-kindness. His teacher needed no less knowledge of the Bible, no less understanding of Christianity and its beliefs—she needed these, but she had to *be* something as well as to *know* something.

Much Teaching Is Nonverbal

A preschooler's vocabulary is very limited, but this fact is not the stumbling block to communication that it might seem. Many of the most moving and important experiences of our lives are beyond description. We often say, "I just can't put it into words." This is the case with much of the Christian faith, even for adults. How can one ever express in words the magnitude of God's love as he accepts and cares for us even though we flaunt and ignore that love? What words can communicate the deep solace during sorrow in the embrace of a trusted friend? What words can capture the quality of life embodied in the out-stretched arms of a father welcoming home his broken and prodi-gal son? The inability to put such experiences into words does not make them unimportant. Their very depth puts them beyond the reach of words.

The ability of a preschool child to feel, to understand, to absorb the inner meaning of experience is not so limited as is his word power. A small child's perceptiveness is often a source of wonder to adults, for he quickly penetrates the façade of "seeming" to the reality of "being." He detects duplicity, falseness, and insincerity and perceives beauty, genuineness, and authenticity.

A child's responses are from the depths of his being. His delight is beyond words as he sees a hopping frog, the rainbow in the hose spray, a bright-colored feather, the vastness of the heavens, the emergence of a baby chick from its shell, or the melting of an icicle in his warm hand. His wordless questions are deep as he bends over a dead pet or watches cruelty inflicted on a child or animal.

The ground for teaching and learning is in present experiences. This is true of all ages, but especially so of preschool children. We do not, therefore, teach preschoolers many of the words of the Bible, which are beyond their comprehension. We attempt to provide experiences through which they can know that love and forgiveness which are a part of God's Word to man. Since the deepest experiences of life are often beyond words, the challenge to the preschool teacher is to act out the Christian gospel.

This need for immediate experience is one of the reasons for a period of play in church school. Play is the child's business. Through play he establishes a picture of who he is and who others are. He finds a place in a group. He relives his joys and disappointments, his fears and hopes. He acts out the life he sees around him. To say that a child is "merely playing" is to say that he is "merely living." The teaching situation is not just the story time; it is all the relations that exist as children play, work, talk, and create together.

Many Avenues of Teaching Are Used

What are we saying about teaching procedures? In the preschool departments of the church school there must be flexibility, sensitivity, and ability to use many avenues of teaching.

Let us look at a session in a preschool department where the orientation to teaching is that described above.

The room and equipment are important. The room has been arranged to beckon children with a variety of interesting activities which do not overstimulate. It is a place where each child is welcomed, accepted as unique, and nurtured in the experience of becoming a person who can love others.

Pictures are hung at children's eye level. The room is arranged with "interest centers." There is a block corner with unit blocks and hollow blocks; a housekeeping center with dolls, housekeeping furnishings, and dress-up clothes for dramatic play; and a quiet corner for books and puzzles. There is a place for growing things: bulbs, plants, fish, a turtle or hamster. There are painting easels with oilcloth to protect the floor, and aprons to protect Sunday clothes. There are two or three low tables with chairs for special activities such as finger painting, playing with clay, and cutting and pasting. In one corner of the room is a large rug on which the children sit for group times.

Warm person-to-person relations are maintained. The teachers are in the room before the children arrive, having completed all last-minute preparations, and are ready to devote full time to the children. A personal welcome is given to each child as he enters. His own name is used in the greeting. There is no attempt to "lure" children into the room with bribes, joking, distraction of attention, or coercion. The reality of a child's reluctance to enter his first group outside the family is recognized.

The children are free to move from one activity to another or to stay with one the entire period. During the free-activity time, teachers are on the alert to notice when an adult is needed to interpret one child's feelings to another, when an adult hand is needed to help, when an adult ear can hear and understand the first venture into conversation by two new friends.

The teacher is ready with a smile, a comforting arm, or a lap when needed. She sees her mission as being that of providing an atmosphere in which the child can build a picture of himself that makes it possible to enter into relations with others and with God. She watches and listens reflectively as children sit at one of the low tables patting, punching, rolling clay or dough. She does not expect the children to "make something" according to adult standards. She knows that working with the dough is relaxing and satisfying, especially for those who hesitate to venture into more social activities.

A teacher sits with children at another table as they cut assorted sizes and shapes of colored papers and paste them onto sheets of paper. No patterns are used, for the cutting and pasting make a "picture" by preschool standards; anything more perfect would be a product, not of the child's own effort, but of copying the teacher's work.

The teacher is aware of the many facets of a child's experience. As she sits on a low chair or kneels, she is able to look level into the eyes of a child, strengthening the child's feeling that "This adult is not too big. She can see things as I do, and talks to me where I am." The teacher attempts to understand the thing a particular child needs to accomplish at the moment, whether it be to leave mother happily, approach another child, or acquire a feeling that "I can do it." She is aware that all children are struggling with something in their lives at any given time, and she seeks to help where she can.

By listening rather than continually talking, the teacher can learn how the child sees the world, how he reacts. She serves as an interpreter of one child to another: "He doesn't like it when you push him." She encourages verbal rather than physical ways of settling differences: "Perhaps if you told him you wanted the truck rather than hitting, he would understand." She does not make judgments about "good" and "bad" children, but tries to understand how each child feels and why, and to help him find acceptable ways of expressing his feelings. She is on the alert for moments of his awe and wonder, sometimes participating silently with a child, sometimes adding a word of interpretation: "I'm glad God planned the world so there are bright-colored leaves, aren't you?"

The teacher knows that no matter how many Bible verses a child may know, if he has not experienced love directly, he will find difficulty in loving God and his neighbor, and in esteeming himself. She is sensitive to the ways in which she can help establish the conditions wherein a child can begin to see: that he can do something he previously thought impossible; that he is accepted as a worthful person; that this is his group and his church; that there is beauty and dependability in the world about us; that we may participate in the care of beautiful and growing things; that mistakes are not irrevocable; that there must be limits set wherever persons live together, for the sake of good living; that an act brings a result and affects other people; that other persons have feelings; that there are wonders and mysteries in the world that set us to thinking.

Group Time Is Simple and Varied

In one class, as the period of free activity drew to a close, the teachers quietly invited the children to finish what they were doing and come to the rug provided for group times. Teachers and children put away blocks, trucks, dolls, and other equipment. Some of the children did not want to come to the rug, and they were allowed to continue to play, provided that they did not disturb the group.

The group time was informal. In conversation some of the interests, concerns, and wonderments of children were lifted up. There were songs and a story. Since there had been a snowstorm, there was conversation about the snow and what the children did on the way to church. The group sang, "The snow is a blanket all soft and all white; It falls on the grass and the trees; It keeps the wee buttercups warm in their beds, And tucks in the brown autumn leaves."[1] Some children asked if they could "play" the snow and the song. While the group sang it again, part of the group acted out snow falling, some were buttercups tucked in snugly, and others were brown autumn leaves.

One child recalled the Sundays when they had talked of God's plan for the growing things, and asked whether they could "play" seeds. Some children curled up tight on the rug while some played the warm sunshine, some the cooling rain, and some the blanket of snow. Gradually the seeds began to unfold, to grow and grow. The teacher asked the children if they would like to voice their "thank you" to God for the wonderful plan he has for the world which includes snow. They did. Then the children took turns looking at some snow through a magnifying glass.

In all "group time" activities, the emphasis is on simplicity and enough flexibility to allow for children's comments. There is a mood of quiet reflection. When these are the qualities of the group time, the rudiments of worship are present, and on these a deepening experience of worship can be built through the years.

This Can Be Stated Theologically

What experiences can the church provide for small children which help to bring to birth the kind of life that is Christian? They may be defined in theological language as the experience of grace, the experience of the church, the experience of man as a child of God, the experience of worship, and the experience of forgiveness.

A child three to five years old in the church can have an experience of love, given unconditionally, by being accepted as he is, no matter how unlovable may be some of his behavior; by being cherished as unique and encouraged to become what he might

[1] By Miriam Drury. Copyright, 1935, by Presbyterian Board of Christian Education; from *When the Little Child Wants to Sing;* used by permission of The Westminster Press.

be; and by being trusted. This is the beginning of an experience of God's grace.

He can have an experience of belonging to a community of faith, of feeling sure that he belongs to that community, and of participating in its shared life. He can learn the privileges and limits of group life and come to feel that "This is *my* church."

He can have an experience of the self as worthful, with a dawning awareness of the worth of others. By being treated as a child of God, he can begin to achieve a sense of adequacy and competence and to see himself as capable of initiating and creating. Secure in this sense of worth, he can begin to identify himself with others, their feelings, and their view of this world.

He can have an experience of the awe-producing factors in life; of standing in wonder before the beauty, order, and dependability of our world; of wondering about the unanswerable questions; and of knowing that there is a Planner beyond the beauty. This is the beginning of worship.

He can have an experience of recovery from alienation, of receiving unmerited understanding, and of being received back after failure or deliberate transgression. He can learn that mistakes are not irrevocable. He can become aware that all persons have negative feelings which need healing, and can share in the process of healing where there is hurt and alienation.

When teachers see such experiences resulting from their work, it begins to be clear that they are participating in the venture of helping small children to understand the Word before they can understand its words, and to grow religiously.

VI

Experiences That Make
a Difference

(GRADES ONE AND TWO)

One of the tasks of the church school teacher that is most stimulating and difficult is that of communicating the faith and message of the Bible. The Christian experience of children and young
people can be greatly enriched if they have a teacher who is himself drinking deeply from the biblical sources of strength and who
knows how to use many teaching procedures in correlation—
procedures which supplement each other and which are related
to one another in a unit of study.

In approaching a new unit of study, a teacher needs to ask
himself, "What do I hope the members of the class will gain
from this study? What purpose do I have in teaching this part of
the Bible?"

The story of a group of first- and second-grade children studying the boyhood of Jesus can give us a picture of how several
teaching procedures were used to meet some rather specific goals.
Many of the procedures described can be used, with adaptations,
in other types of study units. We shall make no attempt to outline
lesson plans, but shall suggest ways in which teachers may use
their own materials with imagination.

Since the lives of children of grades one and two are centered in home, school, and play, the things learned in church school should help the children live constructively in those areas. Understanding how it felt to live in the time of Jesus' boyhood contributes more to children's lives than memorizing facts about Jesus' times. Teaching procedures should be used that make Jesus' boyhood live and put the emphasis on meanings rather than on facts alone.

They Start with a Game

The leader of the group began by trying to arrange a rich learning environment. She knew that all the pictures, books, worship, stories, hymns, and activities must work toward the same goal. Knowing that primary children spend much of their time at play, she decided to start the unit with a game. She asked an artist to make black crayon drawings of articles familiar to Jesus in his home and school. Using a Bible dictionary as a reference, the artist drew pictures of a water jug, cooking pot, water skin, lamp, broom, wheat grinder, carpenter's tools, prayer shawl, scroll, stylus, sleeping mat, and sandals.

The teacher then cut from magazines large pictures of articles with which boys and girls of today are acquainted. She found pictures of a sink, electric frying pan, electric lights, refrigerator, broom, vacuum cleaner, flour, carpenter's tools, Bible, bed, shoes, pencil, and television receiver. The class was divided by two's and they attempted to match the articles of today with the things Jesus knew as a boy. Out of this game came a lively discussion of what Jesus' home, school, and church were like—how they were different from ours and how they were similar.

They Organize for Research

Using the interest and curiosity which the game had awakened, the teacher asked how many of the children would be interested in making a big chart of "Then" and "Now." They would list on the chalkboard home, school, church, and play, and would compare activities in Jesus' day with those of boys and girls today. All of the children but two chose to take part in this activity. The other two met with the teacher separately and decided to gather a collection of pictures of Jesus as a boy as the basis of later discussion and study.

During the next session, the group talked about what activities they might carry out, what trips or interviews might be needed, and where they could find information. During this session, the group thought together about plans—the teacher did not tell the group what it would do. This does not mean that the teacher did not have suggestions and ideas, but she guided the children in planning, giving them as many free choices as possible.

Brown wrapping paper (usable even in the most cramped quarters) was used in the planning. The teacher wrote on the paper WHAT WE WANT TO FIND OUT, and the group listed articles and activities of Jesus' boyhood about which they needed more information. Then the teacher wrote: WHAT SHALL WE DO? HOW SHALL WE FIND OUT?

Various suggestions were noted, such as: look in books, read the Bible, ask the minister, visit a Jewish rabbi or synagogue, see some films or filmstrips, and look at pictures. The teacher knew the list was incomplete, but she felt that another planning session could be held after the interest of the youngsters had been developed by actually beginning the work. The lists were posted on the wall, so that progress could be checked.

A sheet of brown wrapping paper was placed on one wall of the classroom. It was ruled into two columns, labeled: THEN and NOW. The group decided to draw pictures of the articles or activities rather than trying to print. First- and second-graders are very proud of their budding ability to write, and they should be given opportunities to write a few words now and then, but extensive writing is too demanding.

They Concentrate on Homes

The group decided to concentrate on the home of then and now. The next few weeks were spent in gathering information about biblical homes. Four major activities were carried on:

1. Research in reference books: a Bible dictionary, a Bible atlas, and books such as *A Picture Book of Palestine,* by Ethel L. Smither (Abingdon).

2. Viewing of the filmstrip, *Two Thousand Years Ago—Part I, The Home* (from a set of six filmstrips entitled *Two Thousand Years Ago*[1]).

3. Reading and hearing stories about Jesus at home in such books as: *Once There Was a Little Boy,* by Dorothy Kunhardt (Viking Press); *Tell Me About Jesus,* by Mary Alice Jones (Rand McNally); *When Jesus Was a Little Boy,* by Georgia Moore Eberling (Children's Press); *Jesus Lights the Sabbath Lamp,* by James S. Tippett (Abingdon); *Jesus Goes to the Synagogue,* by Helen Brown (Abingdon); and *Pia's Journey to the Holy Land,* by Sven and Pia Gillsater, translated by Annabelle MacMillan (Harcourt, Brace).

4. Research in the Bible for information about Jesus as a boy.

Another planning session was held to see if the group was ready to start putting the pictures on the chart. The teacher used several questions to discover how accurate the study had been: What did the inside of Jesus' house look like? How was it heated and lighted? How did the family sleep? As various children reported what they had learned, they were allowed to choose sections of the chart on which they would like to draw.

They Build a Model House

One of the boys suggested that, since there were too many children to work on the chart all at once, part of the group might do something else. The teacher suggested the possibility of building a model of a home like one Jesus might have lived in. Two fathers came to help with it. Several weekday sessions were

[1] Available from United World Films and from denominational sources, by the strip and the set.

held, and these added to the fun, especially when there were refreshments. Boys and girls had a chance to use hammers and saws, just as Jesus did in the carpenter shop.

Soon a wooden refrigerator crate was transformed into a Palestinian house, with steps that could actually be climbed. Several weeks later it was completed, painted white on the outside, furnished with sleeping mats, clay lamps, and water jugs, all made by the children.

They Study Jesus' Background

When the group working on the chart finished the home section, they moved on to Jesus' school and church. They looked at the filmstrip *The Synagogue*, from the set *Two Thousand Years Ago*, mentioned above. The whole group took a trip to a neighboring synagogue, having drawn up the previous Sunday a list of things to look for. After they returned, one Sunday and a good part of the next were spent in making scrolls such as Jesus might have used in school. These were not elaborate like the ones in the Jewish synagogue, but the parchment paper used made them beautiful and durable.

When the scrolls were completed, the group talked about which parts of the Bible Jesus had known and studied, and each child chose a verse to put in his scroll in careful script printing. First- and second-graders are trained in script printing, so short verses were selected, such as: Deuteronomy 6:4-6; Psalm 9:1; Psalm 24:1a; Psalm 75:1; Psalm 92:1; and Psalm 100:5.

The picture research group reported, showing pictures of the boyhood of Jesus, as various artists had conceived it. Each of the pictures was carefully studied. This helped the children to understand that Jesus was once a child like them. After all the pictures had been studied and compared, the teacher asked if each child would like to have a small print of one picture to mount and hang in his room at home. The group liked the idea and agreed on a choice.

The teacher decided to include a brief consideration of the mezuzah at this point, in an effort to relate what had been learned to the children's homes. A Jewish family in the community lent a mezuzah, and the boy of the family came to explain what the little box mounted on the doorpost meant to a Jewish family and how it was used. The children then made simple mezuzahs for their own rooms at home.

When all of the planned activities were completed, the group spent some time with the "Then" and "Now" chart, adding similarities between Jesus' childhood and theirs. This emphasis on similarities was important, because the differences in household articles and school methods could give the impression that Jesus was not at all like boys and girls today—that his life was queer and remote.

They Make Up a Play

On the following Sunday, feeling that a change in pace was in order, the teacher asked whether the group would like to make up a play about the boyhood of Jesus. She suggested two ways of doing it: by dramatic play, using the model home, household articles, scrolls, and other objects; and by using hand puppets. The group was divided in its interest, so one of the parents was invited to work for a few Sundays with the group interested in hand puppets while the teacher worked with the group doing the dramatization centering around the model house.

Informal dramatization is one of the most effective teaching procedures. In this case, it also provided an excellent way to use the models. The following preparation was made in planning the dramatization:

The story was told enough times for the children to have it clearly in mind.

The group decided how many people were needed and who would play each part.

They decided where in the room each action would take place. They divided the story into sections, like acts of a play.

They talked about each of the characters long enough that the children began to feel how it would be to play that person.

When the group was ready, the children acted out the story informally, letting the conversation be spontaneous. (Pantomime can be used where children have never participated in dramatization and feel self-conscious about it.)

After acting out the story, the group evaluated what they had done, then tried it again, with different children taking the various parts.

All through the series of learning experiences described thus far, the group worshiped regularly. When possible, the leader used in worship a picture of Jesus as a boy, and the group learned several hymns about the boy Jesus. Care was exercised in selecting hymns with good content, as was done also in the selection of stories. In one worship service, the Elsie Anna Wood picture, *Hilltop at Nazareth,* was used. It portrays Jesus as a boy communing with God. The teacher read the passage from Deuteronomy 6:4-6. The children quietly hummed "Fairest Lord Jesus" while the teacher asked them to think about God and how we can talk with God.

Many conversations were held during the worship time about the way in which Jesus must have prayed as a boy, judging from the intimate relation he had with God later in life. Suggestions were made about how boys and girls today might pray individually. Times were allowed for quiet reflection during the worship, so that the children could get the "feel" of quiet individual prayer.

They Invite Parents to a Meal

As a closing summary activity, the group planned to have a meal with the parents so that they could share with them what they had learned. A man in the community who knew about early Palestine was invited to help the class plan a menu which would be very much like one that Jesus and his family might have had. Each family brought a part of the meal, suggestions for recipes and preparation having been provided.

The mothers and fathers played the game which the children had played during the first session, and the children discovered with delight that their parents did not know how to match all the items either. After a sharing time, examination of the model house, and worship, the families went home, each carrying a mezuzah, a scroll, and a picture of Jesus as a boy.

This group had the privilege of taking part in a number of learning situations. As the teaching procedures are examined, it appears that they meet the test of several important criteria of effective teaching.

EVALUATION OF TEACHING PROCEDURES

1. Each was integrally related to the study carried on. No matter how novel or interesting, a procedure is not valid unless it contributes to the insight, information, and growth of the learner.

2. Several enlisted the children in ongoing activity. Learning experiences that continue for several sessions are usually more interesting and significant than those which are completed in one session. Making a model of Jesus' home called for research and offered possibilities for more involvement and interest than would coloring a picture of Jesus' home.

3. Several enlisted the hands as well as the minds of the children. Procedures that use the whole person, including bodily activity, are more likely to produce learning than are those which require children to be quiet, docile, and passive. Discussion is more effective than lecturing. Stimulating a group to find answers is better than telling them the answers.

4. Most of the procedures were dependent on planning and thinking by the boys and girls. Children learn most eagerly when they share in a democratic process from the planning to the completion of a unit of study.

5. Several of the activities were built on what had already been learned. Children like to use what they already know in pushing on to new understanding. Continuity and unity in learning facilitate new thrusts of experience.

6. The products of the group activity were shared with others. Communicating to someone else what has been learned helps to clarify it. A sense of the importance of what has been learned often comes when it is summarized and shared.

HOW PROCEDURES SUPPORT EACH OTHER

A closer examination of the relations of the various teaching procedures to each other is in order. The beginning game evoked children's interest and curiosity, laying the groundwork for the discussion of many spontaneous questions. The teacher did not have to lecture about the articles Jesus used at home and in school—the children had discovered them.

The teacher was at all times an active participant in the group process, but when she introduced suggestions and ideas (as in the case of the chart, the dramatization, and the model), these grew out of the things the group had undertaken.

The planning sessions are as much a part of teaching as is reading a book or interviewing an expert. This group had several planning sessions: to list what needed to be learned and how the group might proceed; to evaluate what progress had been made on the activities and to discuss the deeper meanings; to plan further activities; to plan how they might share what they had learned with their families.

Throughout the study, research was important and was accomplished in several ways. Often teachers feel that the only way to help children gather information is to guide them to books. This method was used, but so were many others: visiting a synagogue, viewing filmstrips, studying pictures, consulting with the fathers concerning the model home, reading the Bible, talking with the Jewish boy who visited the class, and interviewing an expert on Palestinian food.

Each of these procedures was used because the children needed the information that they could secure in these ways. In each case, the information led to further possibilities of activity and work. There was no gathering of facts just for the sake of knowing them.

The worship conversations, and the making of articles to use in their own rooms, took into account the fact that primary boys' and girls' lives are centered in the home. The effort was made to help them learn skills of communion with God, and tangible symbols were taken into their homes to remind them of the experiences which the boy Jesus and they themselves had in common.

As the chart and the model house could not have been made without the previous discussion and study about life in Jesus' time, so the scroll activity was enriched by the trip to the synagogue and the study of passages of the Bible that Jesus might have known. Similarly, the discussion about the relation of present-day living to Jesus' boyhood would have been impossible without the study about the nature of his home, school, and church. The dramatization used the model home and its furnishings to add reality, and would have been impossible without the previous research and study. These two experiences, combined with worship, helped to give personal meaning to what had been going on in the class.

The planning for a final sharing time with families called for review, evaluation, and a choosing of the most meaningful parts of the study for sharing purposes. In this way, the closing event was an integral part of the study and not a "show-off" time.

Out of the interweaving of these varied experiences came the possibility for new growth, new insight, new vision of the ways in which Jesus' life is related to ours. No teacher can ever guarantee that these results will occur. She can, however, plant the seed carefully, leaving the growth and harvest to the Lord of all living things.

Light Through Many Windows

(GRADES THREE AND FOUR)

Teaching is like opening the shutters on the windows of a house. Using one method will let the light stream in through one window. But it is only when many windows are opened that the house comes alive and is enjoyable as a home.

A lower junior teacher in vacation school had been given a text full of suggestions of ways to understand and teach children. Her superintendent was surprised to find that she was employing none of the suggested techniques, but was doing the same thing morning after morning. When questioned about it, the teacher replied, "Oh, I'm leaving out all that stuff about dramatizing and drawing and making things. I don't think we have enough time to teach the lesson, as it is."

Many teachers feel that they are being truant to their commission as church school teachers if they do anything other than talk about the material, for they feel that their task is to tell of the Christian faith. This is a part of the task, but by no means all of it.

To teach is to tell, but it is also to love and to understand, to stimulate thinking and wondering, to provide rich experiences, to extend horizons of expression, to help children use what they learn, and to guide them in becoming active learners—involved, participating, searching.

The use of various teaching procedures is not a luxury just for those who have plenty of time and very small classes. It is a necessity for communicating meaningfully the riches of the Christian heritage.

Children of the lower junior age (third and fourth grades) need a church school that gives them opportunities to develop skills, to do interesting things, to find out how things work—a church school which leads them in new learning adventures. Many windows to the understanding of the Bible can be opened for children by studying, for example, the story of Joseph and his brothers, often used with children of this age. This story offers good possibilities of using several techniques, related to and supporting one another, that provide opportunities for children to learn from each other as well as from the teacher and to learn through actions as well as through words.

Telling the Story Comes First

With the Joseph story, as with any teaching material, the first problem confronting the teacher is to communicate the basic story so that it is understandable and interesting enough to be appropriated by the children. For a good formulation of this story, see *Joseph, the Story of the Twelve Brothers,* by Florence Klaber.[1] Whatever curriculum material one is using, this little book will help in interpreting the story so that it meets the children where they are yet loses none of the tradition as recorded in the Old Testament.

With rare exceptions, telling a story is more effective than reading it. Telling a story is an art about which many books, available in church and public libraries, have been written. These

[1] Beacon Press, Boston.

can be very helpful. It is well for a teacher, before each session, to practice the story several times, until she "feels" the persons involved and can speak as though she were they.

A teacher can supplement the words of a story, thereby enriching its meaning, by involving the boys and girls in ways other than listening. The effectiveness of all teaching procedures depends on the children's having a clear understanding and appreciation of the basic story.

Many Procedures Enrich the Story

An interesting and productive discipline for a teacher, at the beginning of a new unit of study, is to discover how many windows can be opened in communicating her story. The following are a few possibilities:

1. Use some stick-figure illustrations, drawn on a turnover chart, chalkboard, or wrapping paper, to illustrate the events of the story.

2. Record a part of the Joseph story on a tape recorder (or have a good storyteller do so) and play it for the class, instead of telling the story directly.

3. Play a guessing game (suspense can increase interest) by drawing representations of the things appearing in the Joseph story, asking the group to identify them as the story progresses. Some examples are: a sheep; a long robe with sleeves; a man with the sun, moon, and eleven stars around him; a caravan; ankle irons and chains; grapes and a cup; a plump cow and a thin cow; a plump ear and a lean ear of corn; a moneybag on top of a grain bag; a wagon and a chariot.

4. Prepare and present a puppet play of part of the story. A smaller group from the class can work on this simple method of dramatizing the story. Detailed instructions for making puppets are given in Chapter XVII. Probably cloth-mitten puppets are most suitable for lower-junior children.

5. Use guided Bible study with the telling of the story. After a section of the narrative has been given, the children can turn to the Bible or to their books and read a few designated sentences to find the answer to a specific question. The teacher will bear in mind that there is great variation in the abilities of third- and fourth-graders to read and comprehend. Therefore, no reading assignment or individual study should be very lengthy, and discussion about what was discovered should follow immediately so that the children who are slower will get from the discussion what they were not able to get from the reading.

These are only a few of the windows that can be opened to the Joseph story for boys and girls. This story, like many from the Bible, speaks to the experiences of children: of jealousy, of favoritism, of family loyalty and rivalry, of achievement, and of reconciliation. Teaching procedures must be sought which help the children enter into the experiences and the feelings of Joseph and his family, particularly insofar as these are also the experiences and feelings of today's children and their families.

A Teacher Develops New Ideas

The following notes taken from a fourth-grade teacher's class records may serve to illustrate some of the possibilities in this kind of teaching.

Sunday, October 1. At the end of our puppet play, we got into a very interesting discussion as to whether Joseph might have been a "spoiled child" and whether that might have been the reason why his brothers disliked him. From there it was only a skip and a jump to talking about our own brothers and sisters and how we felt about each other. I sensed some realism in the discussion; there was intentness as the children talked about rivalry and cooperation, favoritism and competition, fun and fusses.

Sunday, October 8. Recalling what we had been talking about at the end of last week's session, I suggested that we use the tape recorder today. There were squeals of delight. What I had intended to say was that we would use the tape recorder to try to record how we thought Joseph, Jacob, and Judah felt about their family.

We took these characters one at a time. I asked the children to sit quietly for a minute, with eyes closed, thinking how it would feel to be Joseph, for instance. I asked that they remember how his father felt about him, how his brothers reacted to the father's favoritism, and what they did. Then I turned on the recorder and said to the children, "Now you are Joseph, and you have the chance to put in a diary how you feel about your family. What would you say?"

Most of the responses showed sensitivity to Joseph's feeling: "I get awful lonesome sometimes, because I feel left out by my brothers." "My father is very kind to me and I feel real close to him, but that seems to make my brothers mad." "Lots of times I think my brothers don't like me at all, and I feel sad and wonder why."

We rewound the tape and listened to the Joseph section, criticizing it where necessary before we went on to think about Judah and Jacob.

Sunday, October 15. We found that we needed to do some reviewing in our books before we could "feel" much with Judah, so we made that tape this morning. We decided to call the tape recordings, "The Secret Diaries of Joseph, Judah, and Jacob."

This was my first experience with a tape recorder, and children certainly find it much more interesting than writing a story. Third- and fourth-graders write so laboriously that the whole creative flow of ideas is stopped by the mechanical process. With the tape recorder, one child's idea leads into another's, and the flow is continuous.

Sunday, November 12. Having spent the last couple of Sundays in trying to get clearly in mind the story of Joseph in Egypt, I felt it was time to do something about it; so I suggested that we become Joseph's family back home and decide what to do about the famine.

Before starting the family council, we decided on the things we might have to talk about, such as whether to go back to Egypt for more grain, what to do about the money that was found in the sacks, what to do about Simeon back in Egypt, and what to do about taking Benjamin. Each person then chose which member of the family he wanted to be, and we held a family council—a simple dramatization.

Sunday, November 19. Some of the children had heard on television about a famine in India, where many people do not have enough food. Some pictures of children of about fourth-grade age had been shown in the television program, and my children were very perturbed and sympathetic. I sensed that this was an opportunity to help them find a way to express their concern concretely. I told them about the work of CROP, and how much milk and food a few cents will buy. We agreed to try to earn extra money and save from allowances for the next two weeks, so that, like Joseph, we could do something about the shortage of food in our world.

Sunday, November 26. Ten dollars came in today! We figured out how many glasses of milk that would send to India, and designated one child and her mother to write a letter to CROP, enclosing a money order.

We decided to divide into two newscasting groups: one to give a newscast directly from the radio station of the king of Egypt in Joseph's day; the other to give a newscast from the lower junior department of our church. Each would describe the famine, and each would tell what was being done about it. The Egyptian group could interview Joseph to learn about his plans for heading off starvation among the people.

In the process of working out a newscast, the children turned to their books and Bibles to check facts and find out more about the situation. Their interest and involvement were high as they lost themselves in the process of producing a newscast.

These notes indicate a wise and sensitive teacher, alert to the contributions of the class, yet unafraid to introduce new ideas. The nine weeks described illustrate the manner in which many teaching procedures can be used to supplement one another.

Out of the puppet play grew a discussion of the kind of person Joseph was, which led into a period of self-examination and sharing. The teacher then introduced a new idea: the use of the tape recorder; but it was used to continue the discussion of the Bible story in an effort to get at the feelings of the people in it.

This process in turn called for review and study. The informal dramatization of the family council followed the study of the famine, and the children's report the following week about the current famine in India made possible close-to-home learning. Instead of simply recalling the children to the Bible story and away from their concern about TV information, the teacher helped the children relate the two. Out of this came their expression of Christian concern in their gift of money.

On the basis of this experience of sharing, the production of the newscasts became more than just an interesting exercise; it was real because the group *knew* about famine and had done something about it.

Making Things Adds to the Learning

There are still other windows that can be opened on the Joseph story. Youngsters' hands as well as their minds ought to be busy, and the use of two or three teaching procedures that involve making something is important. Making a frieze of the Joseph story, constructing a series of dioramas, and putting symbolic representations into permanent form are three possibilities.

Making a frieze. The kind of frieze recommended is a connected series of pictures displayed on the wall and depicting the sequence of events in a story. The group lists on the board the various events in the Joseph story. They may do this from memory as long as they can, and then may turn to their books and Bible to find out about further happenings. From the list, each child chooses one or more scenes that he would like to depict. In order that this may not be a duplication of experiences the children have had in public school, the making of this frieze can be different in some way; either the frieze can be larger (two widths of wallpaper pasted together make a very high one) or it can be done in a different medium, such as chalk or paint sticks. Chalk can be sprayed with a fixative when the drawing is finished, to avoid loss of the picture by smearing. "Payons" are paint sticks which give brilliant colors of paints without the messiness of brushes.

Making a diorama. A *diorama* is a miniature stage setting or scene. A medium-sized cardboard box with one side and the top cut away is used for the stage. Scenery is drawn on paper, which is then pasted around the three inside walls of the box. Detailed suggestions are given in Chapter XVI.[2]

Making symbolic representations in permanent form. If the children are interested in the objects appearing in the story, they may like to review the story and either choose some of the things previously used or decide on new ones to draw or paint and frame for their classroom or to take home. Tempera paint—mixed thick, in black, dark blue, or dark green—on white paper, can be used to make a picture suitable for framing. In one class the boys and their fathers worked together, making the frames for the symbols and hanging them.

These activities are valuable teaching procedures. They can give children enough confidence in themselves to produce something worthwhile, a feeling of achievement, a sense of personal worth, and the ability to make a contribution to a group. Such activities require research: looking up the details of the story; hunting for pictures showing what people wore and what their homes and the countryside looked like.

Use New Ideas When Reviewing

The task of finding ways to review what has been learned, without drill or deadly repetition, is a challenge to the imaginative teacher. The use of a shadow play, a one-session mural, and a "Who am I?" game are some of the possibilities.

[2] See also *Aim Your Activities at Teaching Religion,* by Ruth Armstrong Beck (Office of P & D, National Council of Churches, 475 Riverside Drive, New York 27, N.Y.), and *Creative Activities,* by Rebecca Rice (Boston: Pilgrim Press).

After the study is completed, or nearly so, the class looks back over the whole story and decides on the two most important scenes of the story, to be portrayed in a shadow play.

A shadow play requires no costuming, calls for only very simple arrangements (a sheet suspended from a wire and a 150-watt spotlight bulb), and reduces self-consciousness by giving the participants anonymity. The players need to stand close to the sheet so that their shadows are sharp. The light should be far enough from the sheet to make the shadows as nearly life-size as possible. A narrator in front of the sheet can carry the thread of the story as it is acted out in shadow pantomime.

When a one-session mural project is used for reviewing, the teacher places on the wall of the room, in advance, a long strip of blank paper marked off into sections about eighteen inches long. The class recalls the sequence of the story; and as they remember events in it, the teacher writes a brief caption at the top of each section of the paper at the appropriate spot chronologically. Then each child chooses which part of the story he would like to portray. Most of the rest of the session is spent in drawing the various episodes. When all are done, the teacher retells the story very simply, each child standing while his part is told and pointing to various aspects of the story in his drawing.

A game of "Who am I?" is fun and good review. Each child is given the name of one person in the Joseph story on a cardboard, which he hangs face down around his neck. He stands up and gives a few hints of his identity, and the group tries to guess who he is.

Any time a group of children do a creditable piece of work, it should be recognized and displayed. A display of the work done in this unit of study should be arranged in the church vestibule, with posters interpreting it and children on hand to explain or answer questions. An old people's home or orphanage would enjoy a program about Joseph, including some of the following:

a hand-puppet play, a mural display, a series of dioramas, a tape recording, a newscast, and a shadow play.

By no means all of the possible windows have been opened for children's appreciation and appropriation of the Joseph story. These suggestions are illustrative, and demonstrate the importance of a number of related experiences which children can have with any unit of study.

VIII

New Light on an Old Story

(GRADES FIVE AND SIX)

A woman recently said about a teacher who had greatly influenced her: "She was one of the first adults who treated me like a person." What a challenge to every church school teacher this characterization presents! A teacher's primary task is to communicate the unconditional love of God. A child who is loved by other persons has the substratum of experience out of which he can begin to comprehend the good news of God's love.

Every child needs this kind of relation with an adult who accepts him, understands him, loves him, and is capable of believing him into the best he can be. The building of warm relations with children is the first element of good teaching. The teacher who has this capacity to understand and love children, and who seeks imaginatively for new ways of helping children learn, is on the way to becoming an effective teacher.

Children learn in situations in which they are active participants rather than docile listeners—situations in which they are treated as persons and are permitted to think and feel. Children need opportunities to explore, search, reach out, and discover.

They learn as they become involved in making plans and testing the validity of those plans, as they are given freedom to express their thoughts and feelings. It is in such experiences that children can come to understand and accept as their own the heritage of our faith.

To illustrate some possibilities in teaching fifth- and sixth-grade children, let us use the parable of the Prodigal Son. A specific Bible story is used so that the suggestions can be concrete rather than general, but the principles can be applied to any curriculum unit being used.

A Teacher's Preparation Comes First

A teacher's first step is to find out as much as possible about what he is to teach. He will find information and excellent interpretation in the *Abingdon Bible Commentary, The Interpreter's Bible,* and Bowie's *The Story of the Bible.*[1] He will immerse himself in the subject matter so that he knows as much as possible about its background, its meaning. He will ask skilled teachers for suggestions. He will do enough planning in advance so that he can see the whole unit of work in prospect, without planning so rigidly that there is no room for the children to contribute their ideas.

Before beginning to teach, the teacher will ask himself: "How can the members of the class and I so get *inside* the story that it lives for us and becomes a part of our deepest experience? How can I help children to know the love of God to which this story points?"

The First Session Has Possibilities

A recurring challenge to teachers is to make the opening session of a new unit of study interesting and to build on the children's interest in succeeding sessions. This may be done in a number of ways.

[1] Abingdon Press, New York.

1. *Use a radio script.* The use of a radio script is one way to communicate the basic material interestingly yet clearly. It is possible for the teacher to sketch the story briefly beforehand, but preferably the students should read the story for themselves, silently, looking for ways in which it can be broken into speaking parts. The following script, using the exact words of the Bible, was worked out by a sixth-grade class:

NARRATOR:	Luke 15:11b-17a
YOUNGER SON:	Luke 15:17b-19
NARRATOR:	Luke 15:20-21a
YOUNGER SON:	Luke 15:21b
NARRATOR:	Luke 15:22a
FATHER:	Luke 15: 22b-24a
NARRATOR:	Luke 15:24b-27a
SERVANT:	Luke 15:27b
NARRATOR:	Luke 15:28-29a
OLDER SON:	Luke 15:29b-30
FATHER:	Luke 15:31b-32

If none of the children can read well enough to be the narrator, this part can be carried by the teacher, though it is better to have a child do it if possible. In order to involve other children, the radio setting might be made more vivid by having one or two children make a tin-can microphone with class call-letters on it, and by having an "engineer" make and hold up signs saying "Silence" and "On the Air."

2. *Study pictures.* Another possibility is to give each child a picture of the return of the Prodigal Son. Small, inexpensive reproductions are available from denominational bookstores or from Perry Pictures, Inc., Malden, Massachusetts. Two or three larger pictures of this subject by different artists might well be used, so that the children see various interpretations and do not identify any one as the "true" picture. While the teacher tells the story in his own words, each child can look at his individual

picture or at the larger pictures to find the different people mentioned and to study the feelings of these persons as revealed in
their facial expressions and bodily movements.

3. *Discuss the story*. Before the radio program or the art study
begins, the teacher writes on a sheet of brown wrapping paper
the question: "What is the main idea of this story?" He asks the
children to try to figure out the main idea as the story is being
told. The radio script may be reread, so that the details begin to
stand out. By stopping now and then to talk, adding information
or asking questions, the teacher helps to clarify the meaning. He
may speak of Jesus as the one who first told this story, and of
the relation of the father in the story to God our Father.

Dramatize the Story

Dramatization helps children to "live inside" the story
and to experience the feelings of the people in it. When Tom, the
chief mischief-maker in his class, volunteered to be the father in
a dramatization of the story of the Prodigal Son, the teacher had
some misgivings. But these were soon dissipated. As the son
started down the homeward road, Tom spontaneously smiled,
reached out his arms and said quietly but joyfully, "Why, that's
my boy!"

Simplicity is the key to the use of dramatization with children.
They need to be clear about the story, its sequence of scenes, and
the kind of people in it—how they might have felt, what they
were doing, what it was like to be this kind of person. It is important to talk about each character long enough so that each
child begins to "feel" that role, whether or not he ever plays it.
Beyond that, they should be free to enter into the experience of
the characters and let their conversation unfold spontaneously.

This particular story has many possibilities for dramatization:
the division of the heritage, the son's misery in the far country,
his decision to come home, his reception, and the older brother's

reactions. The experience will be most meaningful if, instead of just playing the story, the children who take the various parts will also talk about how they felt. Each scene must be short and simple enough so that the primary feelings do not become clouded with dramatic effects.

Questions such as the following may be a guide to the children in thinking through how they felt:

1. *To the child playing the part of the father:* How did you feel when your son wanted to leave? How did you feel while he was gone? How did you feel when you saw him on the road a long way off? How did your older son's attitude make you feel?

2. *To the child playing the part of the younger son:* How did you feel when you left home? How did you feel as you tended the pigs? (The teacher will already have told how degrading it would be for a Jew to have to care for swine and eat their food.) How did you feel when you decided to go home? How did you feel when you saw your father? How did you feel when you saw your older brother?

3. *To the child playing the part of the older brother:* How did you feel when your brother left? How did you feel when he came back? How did you feel toward your father after your brother's return?

The story can be played several times with different children taking the different roles and then thinking through with the group how they felt. The other children can share in this experience by saying how they would feel in the same situation.

Dramatization is a teaching method which involves children in active participation, discussion, response, reflection, and expression. (See Chapter XVII.)

Use Interest Groups

The use of interest groups is another method of teaching which involves all the children as participants. Instead of having all the children in a department working on the same material at the same time, they are divided into interest groups or committees.

The basic teaching material is communicated to all the children in a department session by the leader. Each small unit then chooses that part of the study which it would like to explore further and express in some way to the whole department on a "sharing Sunday" four to eight weeks later.

This plan gives children a share in planning their study, in choosing what part interests them most, and in working out co-operatively a means of expressing their discoveries. Some possibilities for the interest-group projects are:

1. A radio interview about the story.
2. A newspaper report of the story.
3. Study of art representations of the story.
4. Music research.
5. A "what-if-it-had-happened-today" study and report.

The radio interview project is basically a form of dramatization, based on the idea of the "man-in-the-street" interview used on radio. One child acts as a roving reporter. He interviews the younger son as he sets out on his journey, asking why he is leaving, where he plans to go, and what his father will do without him. In the far country, he asks the younger son what he plans to do with his money. Later, when the son is living in disgrace, he asks what has happened and what he plans to do. When the son is home again, the reporter asks how it seems to be home and what are his plans for the future. The reporter interviews the father when the son leaves, while he is away, and after he returns. He holds similar interviews with the older brother.

None of this needs to be written down, but it has to be well planned and talked through far enough in advance so that the interview questions and the responses are in keeping with the meaning of the story. Several practice interviews must be held before the sharing Sunday.

The newspaper reporting group uses almost the same material, but writes it up in newspaper form, with headlines, human-interest angles, and news stories under date lines from the far country and the home village. A member of the class serves as staff artist.

The art group studies in detail five or six paintings of this story, looking for the way in which the story has spoken to each artist and the particular way in which he has expressed its meaning. The group may want to make a book of paintings of the Prodigal Son for a permanent record. Or the class may display the pictures on turnover sheets on sharing Sunday, pointing out its discoveries about each picture.

Members of the music group interview the choir director or a music teacher in the school or community to learn about music on the theme of forgiving love. They listen to recordings of such selections as "God So Loved the World," "Like As a Father Pitieth His Children," and "If With All Your Heart Ye Truly Seek Him." They may want to become a choir for a few Sundays, learning one of these to sing for the whole group on sharing Sunday.

The "what-if-it-had-happened-today" group studies the parable carefully, looking for the recurring themes: rebellion, isolation and loneliness, repentance, reconciliation, forgiveness, and resentment. Its members talk about whether they have ever experienced love when they didn't deserve it, or have failed to receive love when they thought they deserved it. They make up a story about boys and girls of today including some of the same ideas.

Provide for Worship and Discussion

One of the most important concerns in teaching the story of the Prodigal Son is to help boys and girls understand the nature of God as we know him through Jesus Christ and to develop their own relations with him. Through the years, worship has been one of the means by which this understanding has come.

The departmental worship services can hold up before the children persons who have loved without demanding anything in return, persons who have seen the fault in themselves and found God ready to forgive and help them start again. Stories can be used of well-known persons or of persons from one's own community (usually used anonymously).

The group may wish to arrange for a special worship experience in addition to those which come as part of the regular program. A camp or campfire situation sometimes provides the intimacy in which children are willing to share their experiences of love, forgiveness, repentance, or closeness to God. One group, after a picnic supper and a time of singing, sat quietly while the sun set and then shared the times when they felt that God's love was most real to them. Years later those children referred to that moment of deep sharing as important in their lives.

Worship provides the quiet times when juniors can become aware of God's presence, can seek forgiveness, and can rejoice in the fact of God's help. Guided meditation (questions or statements interspersed with periods of silence), quiet music, and suggestions about the uses of silence help children learn how to use silence creatively.

Another way of getting at the meaning of this story is to discuss with the children *who God is*. They can write down very early in the sessions their ideas of God, and again at the end of the study; they can discuss with their parents their thoughts about God; they can compile a list of the ideas which other people hold. Out of this exploration, the class may wish to talk further about what the expression "God is love" means.

The teacher's aim will be to push beyond the pat answers that many children learn, to get the children to do some real thinking. Such questions as the following may be provocative and indicate that there are no easy answers: Does the fact that God is love mean he is willing to forgive anything anybody does? Does he remove the consequences? Does it mean that God really doesn't care what we do? Does it mean that he is more willing to receive us back after we have done something wrong than if we had never done it? What is the meaning of the older brother's attitude? What does the father's attitude say about God?

Make Up a Different Ending

If the father had been a different kind of person, how might the story have ended? Let the group think up some clues for a different ending. These should be told rather than written, since the mechanics of writing stops the spontaneity, even for fifth- and sixth-grade children.

Make Up a Class Prayer

As a way of reviewing and lifting up the meanings of the story for each child, one Sunday can be spent making up a prayer. As the children recall the work that has been done, with enough time for relaxed thinking, they can suggest things to be included in the prayer. The teacher can write quickly as children have ideas. The prayer can be used in a closing worship service.

Make Up a Set of Slides

After the class has discussed the story enough so that the sequence of events and some of the meanings are clear, all or a part of the group will enjoy making a set of colored slides for a projector. *How to Make Handmade Lantern Slides,* by G. E. Hamilton (an inexpensive booklet), gives complete instructions for preparing these slides.[2] (See, also, the section on "Lantern Slides" in Chapter XVI.)

In preparation for making his slide, each child draws a picture at home of that part of the story which he has chosen to illustrate.

[2] This booklet and all the supplies needed for making slides can be secured from Keystone View Company, Meadville, Pennsylvania.

On the next Sunday, he then traces his drawing on the slide and colors it appropriately with special colored pencils or slide crayons.

A tape-recorded script can be made to go with the slides, making them a sound-slide set. As each child finishes his slide, he can work out a narration for it. If there are children who do not care to draw, they can work on the story to accompany the slides. The use of a tape recorder for the narration adds interest and a "professional" touch to the slide set.

Evaluate the Procedures

Evaluation is an important part of teaching. No guarantee can be given that children in a group with which the suggested procedures are used will become different children. But certainly they will have been exposed to two very important conditions for learning: warm and responsive relations with an adult who is "for" them; and a treasury of potential learning experiences from which a child may choose, saying, "This is for me; this I will incorporate into my own life." A further look at the procedures and their relation to each other may be of help in evaluating the results of their use.

A variety of activities relating to the story of the Prodigal Son has been suggested. Their greatest effectiveness can come as they are related to each other in a unified, cohesive learning experience, not as scattered, miscellaneous activities.

Basic to a unit of study are the teacher's preparation and his attitude toward the children. His concern in using the story of the Prodigal Son must be to communicate, both through teaching procedures and through personal relations, the meaning of God's love.

Through discussion, picture study, and dramatization, the children become personally involved in the basic story. By recasting and rephrasing the story, they look at it from many angles. In the interviews, in the art and music study, and in the writing of a different ending, a modern version, a prayer, and a narration, the children express in their own ways the meanings of the story. The group discussion and research add a dimension of thoughtful reflection about God and the meaning of his love. The discussion must not be facile or shallow. It will serve its purpose only as the children probe for answers to real questions and "puzzlements" about God's love, pushing beyond easy or superficial comments. Worship can enrich the class sessions and give opportunity for quiet reflection on the meaning of God in their personal lives.

The child has many windows opened to him by use of the suggested procedures. In addition to reading the story of the Prodigal Son in the Bible, he can:

1. Read the story as a radio script.
2. Look at artists' paintings of it.
3. Act it out.
4. Talk about how it felt to be one of the persons in the story.
5. Participate in one of five groups expressing its meanings.
6. Draw a slide for a slide set about it.
7. Take part in a campfire service related to it.
8. Discuss what the story says.
9. Talk about the nature of God as portrayed in it.
10. Listen to stories about persons who have shared the kind of love portrayed in it.
11. Create an individual prayer growing out of these experiences.

Through all of these various windows, a child may develop a new perspective on the meanings of the story of the Prodigal Son. Out of the unified cluster of varied experiences may emerge a new relation to the Father God portrayed there, an experience of reconciliation, and a deeper appreciation of the nature of love. If any of these happens, it will be worth all the time, thought, and effort it required.

IX

A Challenge to Commitment

(JUNIOR HIGH)

At no time is creative, imaginative teaching in church school more important than during the junior-high years. Yet, this is a time when teachers fail most to use teaching procedures that challenge the young people and make them feel a part of the church. It is at the junior-high age that many churches lose some of their boys and girls, but it need not be so. These can be years when the experience provided in the younger grades comes to fruition in deep personal commitment to Christ and his church. A junior-high young person's horizons are expanding and his mind and spirit are reaching out, searching. The church must keep pace with this growth by using teaching procedures that help the young people to see the possibilities and the challenge of the Christian life.

Two very important factors are needed in a teaching situation to undergird whatever procedures may be selected. First, there must be understanding and trust between the pupil and the leader. A boy or girl at this age is waging a struggle to find himself as an independent person, distinct from his parents. If the leader of his church school group is a mature person who can accept and understand the junior-high person, he can do much to help the boy or girl through this period of tremendous development. It is of critical importance that junior-high young people, while they are trying to sever some of the ties with parents, do not sever ties with all adults. The leader may, therefore, play a very important role as one adult whom the young person feels he can trust.

It is equally important that there be understanding, mutual respect, and cooperation between members of the group. Each member must have a sense of belonging, must feel that he has a share in the making of decisions, and must have the experience of achieving something worthwhile in cooperation with other members. The aim of teaching is to guide children and young people into a personal experience of the Christian faith. Until the individual learner personally appropriates for his own living the truth being taught, there is no real teaching.

Imaginative use of teaching procedures can lead to an interesting, varied learning experience that goes far beyond the content of the textbook. The relations between the boys and girls, and between each of them and the leaders, can become a field of experience in which the things written about in the textbook come out of the textbook into life.

There is need for a fresh approach, especially with junior highs, in the study of Jesus Christ. Two junior highs, when told that the class was going to have a unit on Jesus, were overheard to say, "Not *him* again!" and "If we talk about him again, I'll scream!" Junior highs must have the opportunity to delve into aspects of the meaning of Christ which they have not touched before. They must be helped to face honestly the questions and doubts that arise.

One junior-high department, which was blessed with imaginative leaders, undertook the use of several related teaching procedures in a unit about Jesus. A student teacher, observing in this group, has written the following account of what happened.

✿　✿　✿　✿

"On the first Sunday, the leader divided the department into three small discussion groups. Each group was given a description of a situation in which Jesus called one of his followers, but the situation was not identified as being related to Jesus. The group was asked to discuss the situation and to appoint a reporter to describe in the first person his reactions as though he had been present.

"The situations were:

"1. You are an older man who has two sons who help you in your business. You are fairly well-to-do and have some hired help. One day a man with whom you are slightly acquainted comes along and tells your sons that he wants them to go with him. What would you think? How would you feel? What would you ask the man?

"2. You are a person whom very few people like. One day a person comes by where you work and says to you, 'I would like to be your friend. Leave what you are doing, and I will help you find something else you would like to do, working with me.' What would you think? What would you say?

"3. You are a person who has always been self-conscious because you are small for your age. Because of the work you do, you don't have many friends; in fact, people mostly despise you. One day a very famous man comes to your town, singles you out from a crowd of people, and tells you that he would like to have lunch with you. How would you feel? What would you ask him?

They Plan a Long-Term Unit of Study

"As each reporter came forward following the group discussions, the leader (Mrs. Gibson) said, 'This person had an interesting encounter about which he is going to tell us.' She probed with questions whenever the reporter seemed unable to go further: 'How did you feel about this person whom you met?' 'Did you ask him any questions?' 'Can you tell us any more of what happened to you?' 'Did meeting him make you feel any different about yourself?'

"After the reporters had finished, Mrs. Gibson said, 'These situations we have been discussing were real ones in which some people met Jesus. Maybe you have already figured that out. Let's look at some slides that portray these scenes.' Slides were then projected illustrating Jesus' meeting with James and John, with Matthew, and with Zacchaeus.

"Mrs. Gibson then turned to a large sheet of wrapping paper and said, 'For the next few weeks we are going to be studying about Jesus and the kind of people he chose for his helpers or followers.' She wrote on the paper:

> What effect did Jesus have on the people who knew him best?
> What kind of people did he choose to be close to him?
> Were there any people who had a chance to follow him and decided not to?
> Were there any 'secret' disciples?
> Were there any rules or requirements for being a follower?
> Did his disciples ever 'let him down'?
> Who are Jesus' followers today?

She asked that two representatives from each of the four regular classes meet with her and the teachers to plan some interesting ways of working on these questions, and a meeting time was arranged.

"Mrs. Gibson told me that she had planned two other things to pique the curiosity of the students about Jesus and his followers, but felt that they had become interested during the session and were ready to move on. I made note of her two ideas, however, and include them here. One was to project eight or ten pictures of Jesus and his followers, asking the students to tell what each represented, if they knew, or to guess if they did not know. The other idea was to use a true-false test, including the following statements:

Jesus' disciples were all more or less the same kind of people.
All wealthy people or those with prestige shunned Jesus.
There were some people who chose not to follow Jesus.

"As I watched Mrs. Gibson and the teachers meet with the steering committee, I became aware that, although free choices were allowed, the leaders had done a great deal of planning ahead of time so that there would be many interesting things from which to choose. After making a couple of suggestions, the young people seemed unable to think of more. They 'came alive' when the leader suggested a few attractive ways in which they might pursue their study of Jesus, and they thought of more ways. The following was the list chosen from the activities suggested:

Make a symbol chart of Jesus' followers.
Make an illuminated scroll of the cost of discipleship.
Make a 'Big Book of Disciples.'
Make a set of Kodachrome slides about one follower.
Make a life-sized mural for the worship area.
Write a *You Are There* script.
Write a collect or litany for use in worship.
Have a closing dinner such as Jesus and his disciples might have had.

They Organize Around Interests

"When the steering committee's report was presented to the department, it was suggested that, instead of the regular classes, they have interest groups, so that while they worked on these projects a regular class group would not necessarily be together and with its teacher, but each person would choose a group according to his interest. Each interest group would have one of the teachers assigned to it as leader.

"A twelve-week period was suggested for the study. The first four weeks were to be spent with all four interest groups working on the symbol chart. Each group was to work separately but add its information to the chart when it was ready. After that, one interest group was to work on the *You Are There* script, one on the 'Big Book of Disciples,' one on the slide set, and one on the scroll. Three young people chose to work on the mural in outside sessions with Mrs. Gibson. The work on the worship materials was left for planning later. At the ten-week point, there would be a 'sharing Sunday,' and the next two weeks would be spent finishing any activities yet undone and preparing for the dinner.

They Make a Chart of Symbols

"As was planned, all the groups worked for the first four weeks on the symbol chart, which was a large piece of un-bleached muslin tacked on a wooden frame (6 x 8 feet). After one had finished its study, it transferred its findings to the chart in crayon. A stepladder stood by the chart for the first group, whose findings were listed at the top of the chart.

"Each group prepared its material for the chart under the following headings: 'Name of Follower'; 'Symbol Chosen' (for this follower); 'Outstanding Characteristics (of the follower) or Events' (in which he participated). One group did research on the twelve who were closest to Jesus. Another studied the secret disciples, Joseph of Arimathaea and Nicodemus. This group later took some of the lesser known of the twelve, since the first group could not complete the study of all of them. One group studied people who were interested in Jesus but did not become actual disciples so far as we know: Zacchaeus, Simon the leper, the rich young ruler, the scribe who asked about the commandment, and those who had other preoccupations (Luke 9:57-62). Another group studied twentieth-century followers: Martin Luther King, Albert Schweitzer, and Martin Niemöller. Stories of other contemporary followers were presented by Mrs. Gibson at worship time.

"The original intention was to have on the chart only one symbol for each follower. Since some of the groups found that there was not room enough to record characteristics and events as had been planned, they created and added other symbols, such as two small thrones on either side of a large one to represent James' and John's characteristic desire for the first places in heaven, a rooster for Peter's denial, and a low-hanging tree branch for Zacchaeus.

"Each of the groups was also asked to spend some time finding out on what occasions the disciples disappointed Jesus. Mark 9:33-35; Luke 9:57ff.; Mark 10:35-45; and Mark 14:33-42 tell about some of these occasions.

Worship Is Correlated with the Study

"Mrs. Gibson, in planning the worship services, tried to help the young people reconcile the pull of high idealism and the drag of repeated failure. She used the fact that Jesus' disciples had similar struggles to help the young people understand and begin to deal with their own conflicts and failures.

"The hymns used in worship were all hymns of challenge and commitment, such as 'Dear Lord and Father of Mankind,' 'The Voice of God Is Calling,' and 'O Master, Let Me Walk with Thee.' The teachers had talked in their meeting about the need for some hymns which express more explicitly the nature of Jesus' call to young lives and the kind of commitment required. They suggested that, the next time they used this unit of study, one of the activities might be writing a hymn to be used with music by Beethoven or Mozart.

Sharing Sunday

"A sharing day was held ten weeks after the steering committee had reported and the department had divided into interest groups. Teachers and students had worked for four

weeks on basic research about Jesus' disciples in making the
symbol chart. The next six weeks, using that information, they
had worked in interest groups—on the scrolls, the big book, the
slide set, the radio script, and the mural. Now the work was
completed and the whole Sunday session was to be used in sharing what had been accomplished.

The Illuminated Parchment Scroll

"On 'sharing Sunday' the first group to report was the
one that had made the scroll. From a printing concern they had
purchased real parchment. They had also visited the public
library and a Catholic church, where they studied examples of
illuminated writing.

"The title of the scroll, 'The Cost of Discipleship,' was done in
illuminated lettering. After that only the first letter of each verse
was illuminated. Some of the illuminated letters included intricate pictures in the square around the letter; some had elaborate
circular designs; and some were vivid with color. The contrast of
the brilliant colors in the illumination with the black lettering in
India ink made the scrolls quite beautiful. When I inquired from
one of the boys how the lettering all happened to be so neat, he
replied that they had worked on it very carefully in pencil first.

"The group described how they spent a good deal of their time
searching for passages in the Harmony of the Gospels which referred to Jesus' requirements for his disciples (Mark 8:34-38;
10:42-46; John 13:12-17, 35; and Matthew 16:24-26; 18:3,4;
20:25-27). Each person had chosen the passage which had the
most meaning for him. The parchment was rolled out on several
tables placed end to end so that the boys and girls could work
on the lettering in different places at the same time.

"One of the boys remarked at the end of the showing of the
scroll: 'It was hard to make this scroll, but it is even harder to be
a follower of Jesus. I had always thought it was pretty easy to be

a Christian until we started talking about these requirements. Now I'm not so sure I'm a Christian.'

The "Big Book of Disciples"

"The second group to report was the one that made the 'Big Book of Disciples.' Two of the boys had made a 2 x 3-foot wooden cover with hinged front and wood-burned title. Each of the other members of the group portrayed the disciple of his choice in some manner (by writing, drawing, or painting). The pages included a biography of Judas under the painting, 'The Corruption of Judas,' by Prell; a large drawing of Nathaniel; a diary of James and John; a poem about Jesus' followers; and a painting of the head of Christ, with a few sentences on 'What It Means to Be a Follower of Jesus.' The book was laced together with leather. After the sharing time, the class took it to the minister for presentation to the church library.

Kodachrome Slides on Peter

"The group that had worked on the set of Kodachrome slides chose the story of Peter. The subjects of the slides were: Peter's call to be a disciple; his confession that Jesus was the Christ; Christ's healing of his mother-in-law; the washing of Peter's feet; Gethsemane; striking out at the high priest's servant; the denial of Christ; talking with the women after the resurrection; and Peter's dream, in Acts, about eating strange foods.

"The interest group worked in two sections. One wrote the script and the other posed for the slides. They did the basic research together, reading the Bible passages, talking about how Peter felt, what this incident meant to him, what kind of person he was. Then they separated and the slide group looked at books on biblical costumes. Each person was responsible for his own costume, though all costumes were brought to the church the week before the photography was done, to be checked against the resource books.

"The script group put into their own words a narration for the slides, writing it in the first person as though Peter were speaking. Members of the group were very imaginative in the way in which they had Peter describe his temperament and his feelings at various points and the effect that Jesus had on him. They recorded the narrative on tape, allowing time between the sections for the changing of the slide. The girl who had been the chairman of the group said they recorded the script four times before they were satisfied with it.

"One of the fathers who had lighting equipment for taking indoor Kodachrome slides met with the group at the church on a Saturday morning to take the pictures. Most of the scenes were posed against a blank wall, though one or two had a suggestion of scenery—trees for Gethsemane, a wall for the courtyard in the denial scene.

The Radio Script; the Big Mural

"How I wish the whole church could have heard the *You Are There* script! The teacher had secured from CBS television a sample script of the TV series entitled *You Are There*, a documentary historical series. The group had spent an informal evening at the teacher's home looking at one of the programs on television to get an idea of the techniques used.

"The group chose to portray the disciples' role in the last events of Jesus' life—betrayal, trial, crucifixion. Four young people served as reporters who interviewed the people at Gethsemane, the court, and Golgotha.

"As in the television program, an effort was made to create the feeling that 'you are there,' with the crowd, with the disciples who ran away, with the soldiers officiating. One reporter would finish an interview and say, 'I see that our reporter at Golgotha is ready now. He seems to be talking to some of the bystanders. Perhaps he can get their impressions of what is happening there. Come in, please.' After this interview, the narrator would interrupt to say, 'Our reporter in Jerusalem has just located Simon Peter. We take you there now.'

"As I watched and listened, I had the feeling of reality such as one rarely gets in amateur dramatics—as though I were really present and living through the experience.

"The painting on the wall behind the worship center, done by three of the young people on weekdays, was completed by 'sharing Sunday.' Permission had been secured from the church to paint directly on the wall with water-base paint. The figures are almost life-sized: a boy and a girl in school clothes, their attention focused outward and upward toward a hand which beckons. Across the top of the picture are the words, 'Come Follow Me.'

"Not having taught very long, I was impressed by the amount of work which each interest group had been able to do in the short period of six weeks spent on the separate projects. I spoke to Mrs. Gibson about this, and she said that the use of interest grouping was largely responsible for the high productiveness. Young people are most likely to be interested when each one has a free choice of the group with which he wishes to work. Also, she felt that working on a concrete project with one's hands, along with the study, created more interest than would discussion alone.

The Closing Dinner

"The closing dinner was an appropriate culmination to the twelve weeks of study. Each interest group took responsibility for one aspect of the planning: arranging the room, table, and decorations; buying food; preparing food; and preparing for worship at the meal. The young people interviewed the minister to find out about foods and table arrangements in Palestine in Jesus' time.

"The young people discovered that Jesus and his followers

would probably have had fish, though on certain occasions, such as at Passover, they would have had lamb. The young people decided to have a lamb stew, using potatoes, onions, and carrots with the meat. They prepared a salad of lettuce and spinach with an olive-oil-and-vinegar dressing. They used dark wheat bread, and a dessert of dried fruits: dates, raisins, apricots, peaches, pears. The beverage was grape juice. Everyone sat on the floor rather than at tables.

"The occasion was made as authentic in detail and serious in feeling-tone as possible. The meal was eaten in silence, while one of the teachers read selections from *By an Unknown Disciple*.[1] Afterward, the group learned some early church chants. At the end of the evening, every young person was given a copy of *By an Unknown Disciple*. Mrs. Gibson explained that this was a token of the church's belief in them and of its faith that they also would grow in discipleship."

*   *   *   *

EVALUATION OF PROCEDURES

The teaching procedures described can be used to explore almost any junior-high unit of study. Part of the value of the procedures to this group lay in the fact that the young people themselves helped to decide what they wanted to explore and had a part in selecting the methods for executing their plans. The young people were able, therefore, to measure progress and evaluate results.

The question to be asked by any teacher in evaluating his work is, "Do these procedures help to bring the young people closer to a personal experience of the Christian faith?" This is a question which cannot be answered easily—if, indeed, it ever can be answered by one person about another's experience. But there

[1] Harper and Row, New York, 1919.

are certain ways in which we come to personal terms with our Christian heritage. Generally, it seems true that an individual needs to rethink and reformulate the meaning of Jesus for him, in his own terms. These procedures called for rethinking. There were preparatory discussions, evaluations during the various sessions, and the closing dinner which helped to make the whole experience vivid. But much of the rethinking took place informally, as the young people carried on their research and creative activity.

There is much evidence that personal involvement leads to more effective commitment than do passive observation and listening. The procedures involved the young people actively. The department was so organized that every person participated in the creation of something and shared it with the department on "sharing Sunday." In each undertaking, the participation of every member was necessary for the success of the joint effort. The responsibility for the success of the program was placed in the hands of the young people.

The variety of ways in which the meaning of discipleship was studied made it less a matter of historical interest and more of a living challenge. The procedures called for a thorough study of the subject matter—the facts, names, geography, and chronology —but aimed further at insight born of putting these things through the mill of the individual learner's mind with a creative objective.

Although the personal involvement of the young people as they tried to express what it means to be a disciple did not guarantee learning, it made for excellent learning conditions and an interesting venture. The cumulative effect of study, worship, creative expression of insights, presentation of the projects, and the final celebration made a cluster of experiences which reinforced, clarified, and built upon one another.

X

No Easy Answers

(YOUNG PEOPLE)

Many new teachers of high school classes in church school say, "Discussion is about the only teaching procedure one can use with high school students, except perhaps individual reading. I'm afraid they would think other ways of teaching either artificial or too simple." Yet this is not necessarily true. The lives of teen-agers are many-sided and full of interesting activities; the church's teaching approach cannot be less imaginative, interesting, and varied than the other ventures in which the young people engage. This does not, however, imply that a class should be offered a multiplicity of experiences of a miscellaneous sort, provided simply in an effort to interest or appeal to the young people. The teaching procedures must be interrelated and aimed at providing a rich experience of the Christian faith.

High school young people are very conscious of the fact that they are no longer children. They wish to be treated as adults, and they react against any procedure or attitude which assumes that they are not growing into maturity. Insofar as possible, the church must, therefore, make the teen years a time for more mature, serious study, dealing with the big questions of life which pose no easy answers. Teen-agers need the kind of group in which they feel free to voice their doubts, questions, and per-plexities. Childish "answers" and oversimplified solutions to their questions leave them feeling cheated and rebellious. To be able to catch a vision of the far reaches of some of the ultimate questions of living (Who am I? Where am I going? What is death? Who was Christ? Is there a purpose in life? How does one find God? Why is there suffering?) is far more important than solving them neatly.

In group life, teen-agers find both a problem and a fulfillment. They are seeking to find their way in a world filled with many pressures to make them conform. They value the esteem of other young people and are seeking to find a balance between in-dividual personhood and life in the group. The church which imaginatively identifies with their struggles for integrity, while holding out to them some clues concerning direction, is acting wisely. It must take full cognizance, in its program, of the nature of teen-age group life and allegiance and of the pull of group activities.

Although adolescence is a time of "declaring independence" from old ways imposed by adults, it is not complete without a "declaration of interdependence"—a coming into a new relation with and attitude toward adults. One of the deepest needs of teen-agers is to find a few adults whom they can trust and with whom they can share the things that matter most. The church has a unique opportunity for offering young people the com-panionship of mature and convinced Christians who are "alive" and open to teen-age concerns and enthusiasms.

The world in which teen-agers live is very different from the world of the Bible. The youth culture and the adult culture of middle-class America do not put primary emphasis on a rela-tionship with God as the central requirement for the good life. Relations with other persons and with things are seen as much more real. To be one of the group, to be well-liked and well-rounded, is considered just as important if not more important than to have a relationship with God. Considerable interpretation is therefore necessary if the message of the Bible is to become meaningful for today's young people.

As an illustration of the way in which the Bible can come alive through the use of several related teaching procedures, let us see how this plan worked with a group studying the book of Amos. A high school senior describes what happened to him.

* * * *

"If anybody had told me a year ago that I would be talking so enthusiastically about anything from the Bible, especially the Old Testament, I would never have believed him. The Alexanders (they are our group leaders) are responsible for it.

"Last September we went to the home of the Alexanders for the opening meeting of our high school discussion group. Right off, I knew this was going to be different from ordinary Sunday school, such as we had had when we were younger. It was informal, and the Alexanders treated us like real people. Several of the young people had said at the end of last year that they didn't know anything at all about the Old Testament, and that they wished we could spend some time this year finding out about it. The Alexanders suggested that we start with one of the first books of the Old Testament to be written. We thought they meant Genesis, but were surprised to find that it was Amos.

We Started with an Opinion Poll

"I haven't done much Bible study, and I really wasn't sure how interesting this would be. But since the others had asked for it, I went along.

"The Alexanders started by asking our opinions on a series of controversial statements. We wrote our opinions, and later defended our reactions in each case. Here are the statements:

" 'God shows his favor to good people by making them prosperous.'

" 'The church, for the sake of unity, ought to steer clear of controversial matters.'

" 'If Amos or some other prophet interested in the living conditions of people were to come to America, he would probably be rather pleased with what he found.'

" 'God desires true worship more than true justice.'

" 'Since America is a Christian nation, God will not punish her, but will eventually cause her enemies to be punished.'

" 'One's religious ideas have to be compromised in the business world.'

"After a lively discussion, the Alexanders helped us find places in Amos which had a bearing on the statements we had been discussing. They told us something about what kind of person Amos was, as well as something about the conditions of his time. They reminded us that a prophet often said things that made him unpopular—for instance, Amos said that the Lord would destroy all the enemies of Israel (how the crowds must have cheered!), and then went on to say that, because the people of Israel had a special relationship to God, they especially would have to suffer for their wrongdoings.

"Then we listened to a tape recording made by one of the men in the church who reads very well. It was a recording of the words of Amos, cut and interspersed with sentences of explanation such as, 'Amos speaks now about the social conditions of his time, and God's relation to them,' 'Amos defines true religion,' 'Amos speaks of corruption and injustice,' or 'Amos speaks to the merchants of his time.'

We Prepared a Choral Reading

"When we met the next evening, the tape recorder was there again, only this time the Alexanders suggested that *we* do the recording. We all listened to our voices on the recorder and tried reading a few passages. Then we heard parts of a record of a verse-speaking choir and decided that it would be fun to try to do this ourselves. (I'm sure that the Alexanders had planned or at least hoped for us to do it!) We read the whole book of Amos (it isn't really very long, and is mostly poetry) to find the parts that would be most interesting to put into a choral reading. We used a modern translation and finally made the following selections:

"'1. Amos' description of himself and his decision to speak truly: Amos 7:10-17.'

"'2. The speeches against the nations: Amos 1:3-5, 13-15; 2:1-3, 6-8; 3:1, 2.'

"'3. The cost of luxury amid poverty: Amos 5:10-12, 16; 6:1, 3-6; 8:4-7.'

"'4. What is real religion? Amos 5:14, 15, 21-24.'

"We were surprised to discover how many times we had to practice to be able to read together effectively.

"The minister heard the tape of the practice sessions and asked if we would give the choral reading as the Scripture reading on Youth Sunday. But I'm getting ahead of the story.

We Did "Encounter" Bible Study

"We had done quite a bit of reading and talking in preparing the choral reading, but some of us felt that it was still 'out there.' So the Alexanders suggested that we try some 'encounter' Bible study to get at the feeling and meaning of a specific passage in Amos. We divided into three groups, taking one of the sections from Chapter V about true religion (5:21-24). In one group each person wrote a modern 'translation' of the passage, trying to put it into language that we would use today.

"The second group tried to write down what might have been the experiences that caused Amos to say these things, and how Amos felt. Most of their statements started with, 'Amos, you feel. . . .'

"The third group wrote a meditation on 'What this means to me.'

"This may sound pretty dull and 'churchified,' but it really was interesting. I had never tried to write what somebody else was feeling or to put the Bible into everyday English. Once we got started, it was easier than it sounded. As I looked around the room, everybody was chewing on a pencil or writing. I think each of us wrote more than he expected, once he got started.

"It was just like a worship service when we read to each other what we had written. The Alexanders thought we might be self-conscious and offered to do the reading, but we wanted to read our own. I think that was one of the first times it ever hit me hard that religion is meaningless if we are not doing something to counteract injustice and suffering—whether we caused it or not.

We Studied Social Conditions

"While we were talking about the conditions in Israel—oppression of poor people, shoddy business practices, and such things—somebody asked what our world would look like to Amos. Most of us thought he would approve of America, and that the world is much better now than it was in his day.

"Mr. Alexander asked how much we really know about the world. He works with CROP, the church group that sends farm products overseas. He had a movie of various places where there is hunger—real hunger. After the movie we all sat sort of stunned, hardly able to take it in. We talked about hunger, and then about whether there are other 'sore spots' in the world that Amos might not look on favorably.

"We decided to find out. We did several things. Some of us read a pamphlet which shows how desperate many of the people of the world are as a result of poverty, oppression, hunger, illness, and discrimination. We called on the director of the work with migrants in our county, on the councilman in charge of a subcommittee on housing, then on a woman who knows about refugees and about the United Nations. We wrote to mission boards to learn what the church is doing and where the greatest needs exist. We saw the movie *Boundary Lines,* which shows how the lines that separate people are created by people, and what these lines do to persons. We looked at some of the pictures from the photographic collection, *The Family of Man,* using them one night in our worship. As they were projected on the wall with an opaque projector, we sat in silence, thinking.

"All of us went one Saturday on a tour of housing in our town —that was sure an eye-opener! I had no idea that there were people who had to live, here in America, in such blighted housing as we saw. We began to change our ideas about whether justice is predominant everywhere in America and in the world.

We Took Specific Action

"Most of us young people were pretty upset by the things we had learned and wanted to do something about them. Amos said that religious rituals don't mean much when oppression is present. We talked about sponsoring a displaced person or family. The Alexanders helped us think about what a big job it was and how much time it would take. We talked it all through, and decided that we would like to try something really ambitious like that. We felt it was something 'real,' something vitally important—not just an activity to keep us off the streets. We could help a family of human beings get a fresh start in life.

We Learned Hymns of Social Justice

"While we were working on the D.P. project, we got to feeling much more like a group. Funny how something big like that can draw young people close together. Singing together helped that feeling, too. Once when we were discussing whether God really knows or cares about the living conditions of people, one of the young people quoted a hymn about how God works through us to relieve the suffering of helpless people. We learned the hymn, 'The Voice of God Is Calling,' and several others. My favorite is 'Once to Every Man and Nation.' Others were 'Where Cross the Crowded Ways of Life,' 'Turn Back, O Man,' and 'O God of Earth and Altar.' Sometimes we sang; sometimes we read the words while the music was played. At other times we compared the ideas of the hymn with Amos' ideas. Once we made up a litany, alternately having the leader read passages from Amos and the group sing verses of a hymn.

We Did Some Creative Writing

"We had such a good experience with the Bible study when we wrote our own ideas that the Alexanders suggested that we try more creative writing. The idea didn't appeal to me because I got poor grades in composition in high school; but it appealed to the others, so I went along. We divided into two groups. One group worked on 'Amos on Main Street'; the other, on 'Amos Meets the People.'

"The idea of the first one was to figure out what Amos might say to our town if he were to visit us today. What we learned from the go-see trip, movies, and interviews helped us. We decided not to follow the outline of the Book of Amos, but to try putting his big ideas into a modern setting. It took us several evenings to figure out what areas we would cover and to get our ideas going. One of the girls types well, so she typed our ideas as fast as they came. Then we read them and put them into better form.

"The second group wrote the script for a panel show. It was like 'Meet the Press'—a group of people asked Amos questions about his attitudes and ideas on various issues, as though he were a prophet in our country. The panel members took the roles of a church member, a tenement dweller, a Negro, a migrant worker, and a high school student. When Amos really lit into some of the things at school that he thought were an 'abomination'—cliques, cheating, and dating just to get a lot of 'scalps'—it got close to home.

We Made Objects for Use in Worship

"One evening one of the boys said he was making air-brush posters at school for a party and wondered if we could do something like that in our group. The Alexanders got the idea right away and suggested that we spend an evening on that sort of thing, everybody wearing work clothes. When we arrived, there were several spray guns filled with white shoe polish and several squares of dark cloth. There were also some wood-burning sets and a large piece of beautiful cherry wood. The Alexanders showed us how to use the equipment, and we experimented with it. I discovered that airbrushing and spatter printing are the same thing. You pin a pattern or letters onto the dark cloth, spray the white ink all around it, and then wait until it dries. When the pattern is removed, there is a design the color of the cloth surrounded by tiny spatters of white.

"Half of us worked on a burned-wood 'focus of thought' to put over the altar, with a paraphrase of one of Amos' ideas on it. The others made a beautiful altar cloth with symbols representing suffering and injustice. We were supposed to take the plaque and the cloth down at the end of the study, but we left them because the words and symbols set us thinking in worship.

We Had a Rhythmic Choir

"Some of the girls and two of the boys formed a rhythmic choir and interpreted our 'Amos on Main Street' symbolically. In case you don't know what a rhythmic choir is, as most of us didn't until last year, it's a group of people who interpret a hymn or poem or Scripture passage in symbolic movements, to the accompaniment of music. We used it in the Youth Sunday service, along with choral reading. Several adults told us it was a high point in the service for them, though they had never heard of using such a thing in a worship service.

We Were Deeply Concerned

"Our closing meeting together was especially impressive. We had a sacrificial dinner. Everybody paid as much as he would have for a good meal in a restaurant, but we had the kind of food many people in the world have every day: thin soup, black bread, and rice. One of the young people remarked that it reminded him of the line in the hymn about 'sharing a wretched crust.' Eating as little as millions of people do every day made us realize something of what it is like to be hungry. We used the money for part of the travel fare of the refugee family.

"After the meal we had a half-hour of silence, with only Hebrew hymns played in the background. As the music continued softly, we worked with clay or finger paints, or tempera paints and brush, expressing our feeling about justice and injustice in the world. The Alexanders said that if we didn't want to try the clay and other things, we could use words to describe our feelings.

"Two of the creations I especially remember. One was a formless lump of clay, out of which rose a hand. The boy who did it explained that previously he had been unaware, unconcerned about the suffering of people in our community and elsewhere—as unconcerned as the lump of clay. But now, through our discussion and our D.P. project, he could see that *his* hand could make a difference.

"The other was a finger painting which had Gothic doors in black, surrounded by dark brown and purple. At one side, surrounded by rays of yellow, were two figures reaching out to each other. The girl who painted it said she felt that until people start bridging the gaps between them, the churches will be dark shells empty of the true meaning of Christianity."

* * * *

As stated at the outset, young people need varied and interesting teaching procedures, integrally related to one another. The learning experience described above grew out of the informal, give-and-take relations between the group and the adult leaders. The adults saw their role as that of suggesting, leading, and giving structure to the group. The young people were able to see that their group was "different from ordinary Sunday school," in that there was freedom and that they were treated as maturing persons.

The Leaders Stimulated Research

The introduction to the biblical material in the tape-recorded reading came after considerable interest had been aroused by the opinion poll on controversial issues. The relation of these issues to the big ideas in the Book of Amos led into an exploration of Amos' thoughts, feelings, and message and their meaning for us today. The leaders set the scenery, so to speak, for the drama of Amos by telling of the background, the people, and the situation out of which Amos came. The group was then ready to search for the heart of the message of Amos. The taped excerpts, forcefully read and tied together with interpretive statements, helped to give the feeling tone and to make vivid the content of Amos' message.

As the group prepared the choral reading based on Amos, they found it necessary to read the whole book. They read and studied because of their need, rather than because a teacher had given them an assignment. They turned to the Bible to find the message of Amos because they needed to know it in order to produce something they wanted to produce. This natural use of the Bible prevents the dull routine of plowing through it because the lesson schedule calls for certain chapters to be read.

Many Related Activities Were Used

The various procedures used were related. Interest was sparked by the opinion poll, which led to research into the biblical message. Without the background which the leaders gave, the passages read could have been abstruse. But the vivid picture of the world of Amos and the dramatic reading of his words gave unity and meaning to the experience. Hearing a recorded verse-speaking choir led to the possibility of doing something similar and to detailed study of the Book of Amos.

The feeling that it was still "out there" pointed up the need of grappling with feeling and meaning. Trying to get at the inner feeling of Amos and the meaning of his words helped to make concern for human need and for injustice today an inner experience for the young people.

Singing, creative writing, and making worship symbols added another dimension to the experience as individuals became personally involved. Designing an altar cloth, creating a rhythmic choir interpretation, and reformulating Amos' ideas for today's world called for more than mere intellectual activity. The whole person had a chance to struggle with new insights, to formulate them in fresh ways, and to communicate them to others. The interweaving of worship with the rest of the experiences made it an integral part of the learning process and not a separate ritual.

Each Activity Added New Insight

New insights about the nature of the world today were gained from movies, interviews, the trip, reading, and letters. The important thing, aside from the way in which each of these activities shed light on another part of the problem at which the group was working, is that the young people were able to do something about what they discovered. To arouse young people emotionally about the suffering in the world, and then allow them no chance to help, is almost worse than leaving them unaware. The teachers filled an important role as they helped the group plan carefully in undertaking the D.P. project. Without guidance from the teachers, the young people might have been too ambitious in their planning.

This teaching process involved an interweaving of many kinds of complementary experiences: gathering and studying information; clarifying and reformulating ideas; worship; expressing in a fresh way the truth for themselves as individuals; action and service; expressing feelings; summing up, sharing, and communicating enthusiasm to others.

Perhaps the degree of interest the young people developed is indicated by the fact that they gave time at home to research and writing, and also held several meetings at times other than that of the regular session.

Young people, through these experiences, came to a new appreciation of the meaning of the Bible, its implications for their lives, and its insistence that religion and justice go hand in hand.

PART THREE

PROCEDURES
TO BE USED
AS NEEDED

IN THE NEXT SEVEN CHAPTERS, SUGGESTIONS are given about specific teaching-learning procedures and how to use them with various age groups. Because attention is focused on the procedures themselves, with less interpretation of educational principles than in preceding chapters, it is important that the principles and goals interpreted in the chapters of Parts I and II be kept clearly in mind in the use of the procedures described. Drama, for example, is suggested not just because it provides an interesting way to learn, but because it can be a means of entering into the experience of the persons studied and portrayed and of seeing their lives "from the inside." Creative writing is suggested, not because it is fun, but because working out original interpretations of the lives being studied can be part of the learner's conversation with Christian history. In that conversation the insights, faith, and convictions of the persons who made that history can be "tried on" and appropriated as the student's own.

So it is with the other learning activities described. They are recommended for use within the framework of basic principles of learning.

The leader should keep clearly in mind the purpose which the procedures are to serve in the enlargement and maturing of the learner's Christian experience and faith, and in giving permanent value to the things he learns.

XI

Review and Summarizing Activities

In the progress of a class there are several occasions when it is well to summarize and review, or to test the acquaintance of the group with what has been studied. At the beginning of a year, it is helpful to the teacher to have some idea of where the group stands in its knowledge and attitudes. Reviewing and summarizing are necessary before most of the teaching procedures outlined in this book can be used effectively. It is necessary to review a story and to have it well in mind before dramatizing it. The making of dioramas, slide sets, and others things in construction activities is likely to be no more than busy work unless review and summary of the ideas are incorporated. Creative writing involves pulling together and crystallizing of information and ideas.

Review and testing do not need to be rigid or unpleasant. When testing is handled properly, it is doubtful whether a class is aware that testing is going on. Children and young people enjoy the opportunity to try out what they know, provided the atmosphere is not competitive. Informal conversation sometimes provides the best clues to a student's understanding of ideas and values and his personal commitment to them.

Review, summary, and testing are used in the church school for various purposes:

1. To enable the teacher to assess the progress of the group and of individuals in understanding a unit of study.

2. To clarify for the group the meaning of what has been done.

3. To form a foundation for further activities and projects.

4. To provide opportunity for expressing values and meanings.

Following is a list of some teaching procedures, with an indication of the age-groups with which they can be used. Examples of the use of some of them have been given in preceding chapters. If an example of the use of a procedure has been given, a cross reference is made and further explanation may not be given in the following chapters.

Activity	*Age Group*
Discussion and blackboard list ..	Primary through high school

(Chapter IV, items 8 and 9)

Shadow play	Lower junior through high school

(Chapter VII, section on "Use New Ideas When Reviewing")

One-session mural	Lower and upper junior

(Chapter VII, section on "Use New Ideas When Reviewing")

Game: "Who Am I?"	Primary through upper junior

(Chapter VII, section on "Use New Ideas When Reviewing")

Research for other activities ...	Primary through high school

(Chapter IX, section on "The Closing Dinner")
(Chapter X, section on "The Leaders Stimulated Research")
(Chapter VI, section on "They Invite Parents to a Meal" and
item 6 in "Evaluation of Teaching Procedures")

Game: "Baseball Quiz"	Lower junior through junior high
Game: "Twenty Questions" ...	Lower junior through high school
Responses to life situations	Primary through high school
Crystallization statements	Lower junior through high school
Teacher plays the skeptic	Upper junior through high school
Pictures with which to identify	Primary through high school
Preference sort	Lower junior through high school
"Times this has happened to me"	Lower junior through high school
Writing a summary statement ..	Some primary and older
Supervised study with questions	Lower junior through high school

Discussion and Blackboard List

Blackboard lists are useful in reviewing and summarizing a unity of study. The teacher will write on the blackboard or a sheet of newsprint the heading, "What we know about . . . . ," or, if the study is not completed, the heading, "What we want to know about . . . . ," or "Questions we have about . . . ." Under the heading can be listed the items suggested by the students. In the discussion that follows, the group can pull together and summarize what it has been doing.

Game: "Who Am I?"

In a unit of study that involves several historic persons, the game "Who Am I?" can be used to distinguish them from each other. Each member of the group is given a large cardboard on a string to hang around his neck. On one side of the card he or the teacher writes the name of the person he is to be, and that side of the card is kept toward him so that no one else can see it. He then gives one hint about the person he represents. For instance, if he is Zacchaeus, he might say, "I am very short." If no one guesses on the first hint, he gives another: "No one likes me because of my work." If no one guesses then, he adds, "One day was very special for me. I climbed a tree on that day." When someone guesses the identity of the person represented, he is given the name card.

In a variation of this game, the student pantomimes the person. The game can be played either by teams or by individuals. If it is played by teams, each team chooses some character it wishes to portray; then one member of the team acts out something about that person and the other team tries to guess who is represented. A timekeeper scores the teams according to the time it takes them to guess, using a watch with a second hand.

Game: "Baseball Quiz"

The class is divided into two teams. Four chairs are set in a diamond-shaped arrangement to represent a baseball diamond. The first team up to bat has its first member sit in the home-base chair, as batter. The teacher, serving as pitcher, "throws" a question at the batter, indicating whether the answer is worth one, two, or three bases or a home run. If the batter gives the correct answer, he moves the specified number of bases, and the next batter takes his seat at home plate. Answering a question incorrectly counts as an out; after three outs, the other team comes to bat.

Game: "Twenty Questions"

A good way to test the acquiring of information is to use the old game of Twenty Questions. The class divides into two teams. Then each team looks through the textbooks for names of persons, places, and events about which the class has studied. When one team is ready, the other team has to establish, by asking questions, whether a person, place, or event has been selected. Then the questioning team try to find out who or what it is by asking twenty questions or less. All questions must be so phrased that they can be answered with "yes" or "no." If the team guesses with less than twenty questions, it wins that round and then tries to stump the other team.

Responses to Life Situations

The teacher tells, or records on tape, stories about vivid life situations involving children or young people the same age as the members of the class. Each situation includes a problem or conflict. The group is then asked: "What is happening to the people in this situation?" "Has this ever happened to you?" "What would you do?" In the reactions, the teacher sees clues to the feelings, convictions, and experiences of individuals and some indication of whether the values he has been teaching are making a difference in the attitudes of the children or young people.

Crystallization Statements

Members of the group write brief statements (five sentences or less) of summary, along the lines suggested by such questions as: "What is the big idea of what we have been studying?" "What is the most important thing about which we have talked?" "What has struck you most about our study?" In the case of children younger than fifth grade, the group should talk over their ideas and the teacher write down their conclusions.

Such questions are especially useful after having a visitor, taking a trip, or using a motion picture, a record, or a vivid story. The teacher says, "Write down (*or* tell me, *for younger children*) in one sentence what you think the record (movie, visitor) was saying." The replies guide the teacher in planning future sessions, since they indicate the students' understanding of what was said and, often, their attitude toward it.

Some teachers use a similar procedure in which they ask students to define certain terms in not more than three sentences. One high school group, at the beginning and at the close of the year, is given sheets of paper on which are several words or phrases having to do with the Christian faith, such as *God, the Bible, salvation, grace, sin, atonement, incarnation, trinity, Jesus of Nazareth,* and *Jesus Christ.* The members write their definitions of these phrases at the beginning of the year and again at the end. The teacher of another class makes a slightly different approach by asking, not for definitions, but for statements of personal belief with regard to each of the words or phrases.

A teacher may want to collect the statements and weave them into a litany, a psalm, or a meditation. When this is done, permission of the students should be secured for the use of individual statements.

Teacher Plays the Skeptic

As a means of assessing both the factual knowledge and the understanding of the meaning of facts acquired by members of the class, the teacher plays the role of an unbelieving skeptic or of a person wholly ignorant of what the class has been doing. He asks questions, pressing for proof, reasonable interpretation, and convincing support of statements: "How do you know?" "How can you be sure?" "What does this really mean?" "Is this something we can live by?"

Young children would be dismayed at having their teacher turn the tables on them, but juniors, junior highs, and young people find such an approach stimulating. The teacher must know his group well and have a relationship of trust established with the members before using such a method. Basically, the purpose is to press the members of the group to examine their reasons for thinking as they do, and to find sound reasons for their conclusions.

Pictures with Which to Identify

Pictures can be used in summarizing and testing. One way is to show, at the end of a unit of study, a picture that embodies in some ways but strongly denies in others the basic meaning of what was studied. The group examine the picture, then tell how they think it expresses or denies the idea developed in the study.

Another possibility is to present a series of pictures that show people in various situations and with shades of feeling (sad, joyous, puzzled). The students give their reactions, indicating which persons they feel nearest to, which they feel farthest from, and which are like someone they know.

One teacher used a series of pictures and asked the class to indicate which one was the best and which one the poorest representation of what the group had been studying.

Such indirect testing of the students' sense of values and of the meaning of the study is enjoyed by members of a class as a fun activity. Yet the results often tell a teacher whether each student has understood the point of what he has been studying, and whether he feels closely identified with the attitude or value that has been taught.

Preference Sort

One of the most stimulating methods of helping students to sort out and clarify their ideas is the *preference sort*. It may take many forms, but basically it consists of sorting a number of statements, varying from one extreme to the other about any particular subject. Each student is given a set of slips of paper, each containing a statement, and is asked to sort them into piles. If three piles are used, the first pile is for the slips on which there are statements the person believes. The next pile is for those about which he has no strong feelings. The third pile is for those that he rejects. If there are five or seven piles, rather than three, there are more gradations in preference but the principle is the same.

The process is made more difficult and more interesting if a very limited number of slips is allowed in the first and last piles. If, for example, there are fifteen slips to be sorted into three piles, it is best to suggest that there be only three in the first and three in the last pile, thereby forcing the student to eliminate and choose between shades of meaning. The plaintive comment may be, "But I have too many in my first and last piles!" It is precisely this situation that helps the student to decide which statement he most identifies with and which least.

The subjects of the preference sort can vary greatly: qualities I like best in a teacher; Bible verses or pictures that best portray the meaning of love; the best paintings of Jesus; what a boy or girl of ten years should be expected to do; what I believe; what parents of teen-agers ought to do about a certain situation.

"Times This Has Happened to Me"

Now and then, especially in a camp or retreat setting, there is a depth of group feeling that makes it appropriate to have a sharing of personal experiences. A feeling of "at-homeness" on the part of every member of the group is necessary, along with a basic trust in the leader. Otherwise, members will not share their intimate feelings and experiences and either will not participate or will do so flippantly.

A junior group, while studying the story of the Prodigal Son, had such a session almost by chance. One of the girls started it by saying, "I can remember that one time when I was very small and had done something wrong, my father treated me just like that." She went on to tell about the experience in detail. The teacher asked whether anyone else could remember instances of undeserved love. Some of the experiences reported were humorous, but all were personally meaningful and were treated with respect by the teacher and the group.

This conversation involved one of the most important, yet indirect, forms of summarizing and testing. It revealed the extent to which members had actually understood what the class had been studying and could put it into words so that the others could participate in the experience.

Writing a Summary Statement

(For an explanation of this procedure, see the section on this subject in Chapter XII.)

Supervised Study with Questions

The use of Bibles or resource books in a supervised study period can be a good review activity. Usually the study is most fruitful if the teacher gives the group some questions to answer as a result of their study. Now and then the group itself may formulate questions to which they want to find answers. The teacher will direct them to the study material appropriate for discovering the answers.

XII

More Learning Through Creative Writing

In preceding chapters mention has been made of the importance of meaning in learning, and of each individual's finding his own meaning rather than adopting the teacher's. When something has been especially meaningful to the learners, creative writing is an effective way by which they can express, in an orderly and original way, what it has meant. For instance, a group of high school young people spent a year together in the study of the life of Jesus. At a retreat at the end of the year, each wrote a statement of intention on the theme, "My life in the light of Jesus." During the year there had been glimpses of the meaning of Jesus as Christ. At the retreat stronger convictions were built through Bible study, silent meditation, discussion, and worship. Writing a statement of intention placed on each individual the discipline of formulating his own convictions about Jesus and expressing them in an original manner.

Although creative writing is used primarily to crystallize and express the meaning of what is learned, it is useful, also, as a tool in recasting the content of a unit of study in a new form. A fifth-grade class worked out the following choral reading as a result of their study of a unit on the story of the Bible. The teacher initiated the activity as a review. It is apparent, however, that the meaning of the unit, as well as the facts, was expressed.

KEY: L = leader; 1. = first voice, 2. = second voice, and so on.

L. Years and years ago
      Man began to keep records.
  1. He told stories around campfires.
  2. He painted pictures to stand for words.
  1. He carved on stone.
  2. He penned on scrolls.
  1. He listened to other men talk.
  2. He fashioned wood to tell a story.
ALL: Man was important!
L. Years and years ago
      Man heard God speak
  1. Through Abraham and Isaac,
  2. Through Jacob and Joseph,
  3. Through Moses and Joshua,
  4. Through Isaiah and Jeremiah.
ALL: Through the still small voice of conscience men heard!
L. Years and years ago
      God spoke more clearly through a carpenter.
  1. Selfish people became unselfish.
  2. Proud people became humble.
  3. Hard people became forgiving.
  4. Sad people found joy.
  5. Sick people became well.
  6. Frightened people became brave.
  7. People who hated, learned to love.
ALL: Men were changed!
L. Years and years ago
      Men wrote the stories of Jesus.
  1. Mark's book was short.
  2. Matthew added more of Jesus' teaching, preaching, and helping.
  3. Luke's book improved the record.
  4. John's story pointed the way—
ALL: Man's way to God!

L. Years and years ago
   Christian churches spread
 1. To big countries and little countries,
 2. To new countries and old countries,
 1. To hot countries and cold countries.
 2. Now Christian people of
   all races,
   all colors,
   all ages
ALL: Hear the call and gather to worship.

Creative writing includes a wide variety of activities, from the simple "stories" made up by preschool children ("We went to church today; we saw our mommies and daddies and the minister.") to poems, choral readings, and meditations created by young people. It includes the expression of individual or group ideas, feelings, or experiences.

Children three and four years old delight in hearing read back to them a rhythmic chant that they have created and their teacher has written down. A four-year-old was singing to himself, "We're at church, we're at church, and we like our church. La la la la la la." His teacher waited until later in the morning when he asked her to read a story. She said, "I can read a song you made up." She read to him from her note pad the words of his song while his eyes danced in wonder. "How did you know I said that?"

Five-year-olds enjoy dictating a "story" to their teacher about things the group has done. One such story went, "We took a walk this morning. We saw new grass and tulip shoots. A bunny rabbit ran across the church yard. We heard birds singing. We said a thank-you prayer." The story was written in large printed letters and posted in the room for the children to see.

Creative writing can take place even though the children do not actually do the writing. Even older juniors sometimes create faster and more freely if they are not hampered by the necessity of transcribing their thoughts. The emphasis should be on creating the thoughts, with the writing done by the teacher or a helping teacher.

With children of fourth grade and older, the teacher helps start the thinking by asking questions. As the ideas begin to flow, he (or a helper) jots down the children's contributions. It is difficult to help the members of the group move along in their thinking while they or the leader has to write. Two teachers can work together effectively.

Creative writing is an expressive activity and flows most easily out of situations in which there is a wealth of ideas and feelings.

Children and young people need encouragement in saying things the way they feel them rather than according to adult expectations. Trite phrases can be eliminated if the teacher helps members of the group express ideas in fresh ways. "That's one way to say it—can you think of another? How would it be to say it like this?" The aim is not to find slangy expressions but to find ways that the students talk when they are not in church school.

When the writing is finished, it may be used in any of a number of ways. Older juniors, junior highs, and senior highs may use it as a choral reading in worship. Children may take copies home to parents. A copy may be posted on the wall of the classroom or in a central display case of the church. The teacher should be prepared to duplicate the writing of children if it is even moderately successful, because each child will probably want a copy. Young people may make their own copies.

The following indicate some of the possibilities of creative writing:

Writing a newspaper—older junior and junior high.

Creating a statement of belief (creed)—primary through high school.

Creating a prayer—preschool through high school.

Writing a collect—junior and senior high.

Writing a litany—primary through high school.

Writing a script for slides or pictures—lower junior through
high school.

Writing a radio script—upper junior through high school.

Writing a diary or monologue—lower junior through high
school.

Writing a choral reading—high school.

Interpreting Bible study—junior and senior high.

Writing a psalm—primary and junior.

Writing a summary statement—some primary and older.

Writing a Newspaper

Writing a newspaper account of events and persons of a
unit of study is an interesting activity for older juniors and junior
highs. On the day when such an activity is suggested, the teacher,
if possible, brings to class several copies of the local paper, and
the members of the group analyze headlines, layout, and style.
Then they decide which features they would like to include in
their newspaper.

The Palestine Chronicle was the name of a newspaper published by a class of fourth-grade children as a result of a two-
month study of a biblical unit. The paper was not published until
the end of the study, but various committees worked through the
six months. There were committees on cartoons, advertisements,
biography or human interest, news stories, recipes, and home-
making. After each session, the class decided which committee
could most appropriately work on the material discussed that
morning. The committee came half an hour early the next week
to talk about the subject. The teacher jotted down notes as the
group talked, then brought them back typed the next week for
criticism and rearrangement. The committee on advertisements
worked the shortest time but was a very lively group, consulting
resource books and a Bible dictionary to figure out what items
might have been for sale, what might have been lost and found,

and what employment opportunities might have been open. After they had composed their column, the committee dissolved and the members worked on other committees.

Another class, not so ambitious, used the newspaper approach occasionally for one Sunday only. Now and then the teacher suggested that each child compose a headline that might appear over a report of the material just studied, or that together they report what they had learned in the form of a news story.

One class divided into smaller groups to think up questions that a reporter might use if he were interviewing someone about the material studied that Sunday. The next week a member of one small group interviewed a member of another small group, asking the questions prepared by his group. This continued until all the questions had been used.

Once a year, or every other year, near the close of the church school year, some older junior and junior high groups enjoy preparing a department newspaper. Events of the year are reported by various members. Several features are included, such as an interview with one of the teachers, a news column about members of the group, and a "coming attractions" column on next year's activities. This kind of undertaking has many by-products: heightened group morale, a review of the year's achievements, and participation by many of the members.

Creating a Statement of Belief (Creed)

In a creed, a group attempts to put into writing what the members believe. Such a statement may include belief in God, Jesus, the church, and prayer. Or it may deal with matters of everyday life, for in ordinary living one operates on a set of beliefs or assumptions. The statement may include content such as: What we believe about playing fair (justice), about being good neighbors, and about people. Care must be taken to avoid making trite affirmations. Often, if a child or young person is asked to explain what he means by a statement, his explanation is more down-to-earth than the original statement. The teacher can create a climate for the work by giving examples that are closely related to the everyday life and language of the members of the group.

Creating a Prayer

Both children and young people need opportunity for practice in formulating their ideas in prayer. Learning to formulate spontaneous prayers is important and is a good departure from using rote prayers; but the discipline of formulating a prayer that is worth being preserved in writing is also important. We need help in understanding that we can engage in prayer at any time or place rather than only in church. The teacher will seek occasions and events in the lives of the students, therefore, that occur outside of the church but that call forth an attitude of meditation, thought, wonder, perplexity, or awe. Some examples may be:

1. Young people in the class know someone who has had a death in his family. They wonder and talk about it, then write a prayer.

2. The teacher poses for consideration an imaginary but plausible child or young person who is not liked because he is a show-off; then he asks what kind of prayer might be offered for him without the group becoming self-righteous.

3. A story, a walk, or a picture reveals something of the beauty and orderliness of the world. Appreciation makes this a time to create a prayer of thanks.

4. A child is moving away and the members of the class talk about what they would like to say to God about him. Memories of good times together are recalled and hope is expressed that he will make new friends and not be lonely.

5. A young person makes a mistake, premeditated or other-

wise, that has serious consequences for others. The class talks about the situation, then pauses to let each recall in his own mind some incident in which his own actions may have caused other people difficulty. Then they write a prayer for forgiveness. The emphasis is on helping the group see how all people make mistakes, do wrong things, and need to be penitent.

Writing a Collect

A *collect* is usually a prayer in one sentence. The classic collect is:

> Almighty God, unto whom all hearts are open, all desires known, and from whom no secrets are hid: cleanse the thoughts of our hearts by the inspiration of thy Holy Spirit, that we may perfectly love thee, and worthily magnify thy holy name; through Jesus Christ our Lord. Amen.

The prayer has three parts. There is the opening or address, "Almighty God, unto whom all hearts are open, all desires known, and from whom no secrets are hid." The central idea is contained in the body of the prayer. Then there is the closing in the words "through Jesus Christ our Lord. Amen."

The group works over the ideas they wish to express until they can put them in one sentence. This requires elimination of unnecessary phrases and a clarification of what they wish most to say. Because the collect is brief, it may be most meaningful if written individually, although an initial group composition may be a useful guide.

Writing a Litany

A *litany* is a responsive prayer, usually with alternate parts read by the leader and the group. While in a collect an idea is reduced to a single sentence, in a litany one idea is elaborated into many sentences. The group response usually conveys the kernel of the litany, the major idea. For instance, in a litany of thanksgiving the response may be, "We give thee thanks, O Lord," and in a litany of petition it may be, "We pray thee, our Father," or "We ask you to help us, O God."

A worshipful litany can be composed by a whole group. A junior camp group at vespers one evening was asked by the worship leader to indicate the things they liked best in camp. The answers came slowly at first, then rapidly: the food, new friends, the games, overnight hikes, cooking supper over an open fire, sunsets over the lake. The leader then said, "We are going to make a prayer of thanks for the things you have mentioned. When I pause, you will sing the chorus of the hymn we have been singing, "Lord of all, to Thee we raise, this our hymn of grateful praise." The leader then led the group in the following prayer:

> Let us give hearty thanks to God our Father for our camp, for the good food and the fun around the tables, for the new friends we have made here.
> Lord of all . . . .
> For baseball, dodgeball, kick ball, and the other games we have played together,
> Lord of all . . . .
> For the adventure of sleeping out under the stars, hiking until our feet are sore, the smell and taste of hamburgers fried over the campfire,
> Lord of all . . . .
> For the quiet sense we feel as the sunset turns the lake into different colors and we feel close to thee, O God,
> Lord of all . . . .

Although the group participated in the creation only by naming the categories to be included, making and using the litany was a worship experience in which each felt he had had a part.

Full participation includes sharing in the decision about the kind of litany to be composed, in the creation of the various petitions and the group response, and in its use. The teacher should have available for reference several examples of litanies. After the class has read them and looked carefully at their distinctive features, they decide on a theme (thanksgiving, intercession, or petition for forgiveness) and list on the chalkboard the major ideas that should be included. They decide on an appropriate response. (The response may be sung, spoken, or given in silence. Usually it is spoken.) The actual wording of each petition may best be done by groups of two or three. Each small group brings its idea for the wording, and the whole class evaluates, changes, or accepts the suggestions. When the litany is complete, a leader is chosen and the group uses it, or it may be shared with another class or department.

Writing a Script for Slides or Pictures

Children or young people may like to create a script to accompany a slide set, a turnover chart, or a box movie. They will want to have before them a list of the scenes for which a narration is needed. The teacher may ask questions that cause the group to think about what happened in a particular scene, who was involved, what the important point is, and how it can be stated most interestingly. The teacher writes down the ideas as they are suggested and reads them to the class for evaluation, rephrasing, and elimination; then he types a copy for each child before the next Sunday. In a group of young people, one of the members can do the writing.

Although the reading of the script demands a good reader, many can participate in its creation.

Writing a Radio Script

In Chapter XVII suggestions are given for creating a radio play. Usually informal dramatization of a story in radio form is sufficient, but groups sometimes enjoy writing the script. The process is much the same as for all dramatization. The group must have the story and characterizations clearly in mind, discuss ways to begin the radio play, decide what scenes should be included, and decide how to end it. The teacher may write down the suggested dialogue and action, at the same time stimulating the flow of ideas. A radio script created by a fifth-grade class is a sample of what a group of children can do.

JOHN WESLEY

A Radio Play

Created by a Fifth-Grade Class

LEADER: The time—the eighteenth century.
The place—England.
The times were crying for a leader.

ALL: Was a leader so important?

LEADER: Yes, indeed, because—

VOICE 1: The masses were in deep poverty and shamefully neglected.

VOICE 2: Many changes were needed in the church.

VOICE 3: Lawlessness and crime were increasing.

ALL: And the man to answer the cry was—

LEADER: John Wesley.

ALL: Tell us about him.

VOICE 1: He went to Oxford. He and other students met to help each other in their studies and religion. Some people made fun of them and called them the "Holy Club." Later they were called Methodists.

VOICE 2: He had a brother Charles who wrote many hymns. John and Charles went to Georgia as missionaries to the settlers and Indians. Although the trip was unsuccessful, it was important in their lives. They longed to be like some missionaries they met there whose lives were noble and peaceful.

VOICE 3: When they returned to England, a religious experience came to Charles in a sickness and to John in a church meeting. From then on John wanted to better the lives of others. The world was to be his parish.

ALL: Did not most of the clergymen of the Church of

England refuse to permit John Wesley to preach in their churches?

LEADER: Right you are. His religion was too democratic for them.

VOICE 1: It was open to coal miners as well as kings and lords.

VOICE 2: He taught that God is the father of all men.

VOICE 3: And that before God all men are equal and can be saved.

ALL: Then where did he preach?

LEADER: He preached in the open air.

VOICE 1: In the fields—

VOICE 2: On the highways—

VOICE 3: He did this for more than fifty years.

ALL: His life must have had many hardships.

LEADER: It did, indeed.

VOICE 1: He traveled usually on horseback over bad roads and in all kinds of weather.

VOICE 2: At times he lived on bread alone.

VOICE 3: And slept on bare boards.

ALL: He reminds us of the apostle Paul.

LEADER: Very much.

VOICE 1: He has been called the greatest apostle since St. Paul.

VOICE 2: On the flyleaf of his New Testament he had written the words, "Live Today!"

ALL: Let us be grateful to God for men like John Wesley.

LEADER: The time—the eighteenth century.

The place—England. A new England was coming to birth because the times were granted a leader—John Wesley.

Writing a Diary or Monologue

Penetrating into the inner life of a person of the past, to learn how he felt and why he did what he did, is difficult. One way to do it is by writing a diary of that person. For example, if we could find the diary of Judas, what might it unfold? Or if we could listen to the musings of Saul or Stephen, Moses or Amos, what might they say?

A monologue may involve a sequence of events, or it may center around only one, such as that of the rich young ruler talking to himself as he went home after seeing Jesus.

The success of this sort of venture depends on the group's having a vivid picture of the persons and events, and also on the teacher's being able to pose provocative questions to help the students "feel into" the person about whom they are writing.

Writing a Choral Reading

A choral reading is a script written so that two or more voices can read it antiphonally, in unison, and as solo voices. Variation in timbre (quality and depth) of voices makes an interesting contrast, but is not necessary for most uses of choral readings in church school. An example of a simple choral reading was given early in this chapter. One written by young people is given below. Junior-high and senior-high young people have ability to work out good choral readings if they have opportunity to see several examples and if the material about which they are to write is interesting to them. The following example is part of one that was written by an adult counselor of a group of young people after talking with several members of the group about the situations that made it hard for them to be themselves. It is the kind of material that a group might study when thinking of writing a choral reading. Further help in writing and producing choral readings can be had from books listed at the end of this chapter.

IT'S HARD TO BE YOURSELF

KEY: L = Leader, C = Chorus

L: Do you ever get the feeling of being completely surrounded? Of having people coming at you from all directions, with suggestions, orders, ideas, pressures?

C:	It's hard to be yourself. It's hard to know who yourself is.
L:	Take school, for instance. The teachers say:
2 VOICES:	The grade you get on this test will determine your term grade.
L:	And the kids say:
SOLO:	Lemme see your paper—I didn't have a chance to study last night.
SOLO:	Aw, come on, be a pal. What's the matter? You scared to help a friend?
SOLO:	All A's! What a grind! I hear his mother's a good friend of the principal.
SOLO:	Did you hear about Joe? Poor fellow got straight A's—but then, all he ever does is study and go to current events lectures.
L:	School's the place to learn, they say, to prepare for life later, for college and for what you want to be. But the pressures get sort of strong, and . . .
C:	It's hard to be yourself. It's hard to know who yourself is.
L:	If you're interested in world affairs, and want to talk seriously, you're an intellectual. If you're not, the teachers say you do sloppy work, and how can you expect to live in today's world if you don't read the newspaper?
2 SOLOS:	What's the answer? What's the answer?

. . . .

SOLO (stern):	College Board examinations will be given next week. All those getting high marks will be eligible for entrance into any university without entrance exams.
SOLO:	Be like the rest of the kids! Come on, you don't have to study. You can get by. Live! Have a good time! Anyway, who wants to be a square?
C:	It's hard to be yourself. It's hard to know who yourself is.

. . . .

L:	If you're on one of the teams at school, you sure can feel the old pressures closing in on you! You hear the coach saying:

BOY:	We're the champions, fellows. Let's go out there and keep that reputation!
L:	You see members of your own team committing fouls and getting away with it.
GIRL:	Go, team, go. Ya gotta win! Yea, team!
BOY:	I guess the most important thing is to win. After all, if I don't take advantage of the opportunity, our opponents may, and we may lose.
L:	Clean sportsmanship is there—sure—and training and discipline. But I sure get the feeling that we're not playing the game for the sake of the game. We're playing the game for the sake of winning.
C:	It's hard to be yourself. It's hard to know where you stand, and what to stand for.

. . . .

L:	One thing that really burns me up is the Yearbook write-ups. You know what I mean? I know lots of kids who go out for school activities just so they can have several lines in the Annual after their names. Now, I ask you, if you aren't interested in something, why does it matter to have that activity listed after your name?
BOY:	I heard that business firms, when they are looking over the graduates, look more at your activities than they do at your grades. They want to know if you're "well-adjusted."
GIRL:	I don't think it's fair. The same ones seem to end up doing everything anyway.
L:	Seems like being yourself doesn't count much— what does count is trying to be a big wheel, getting your name on the roll of as many activities as possible, so you can get a big squib in the Yearbook.
C:	It's hard to be yourself. It's hard to know where you stand, and what you stand for.
L:	There's one thing none of us can get away from, but I guess the boys feel it more than the girls. That's the kind of world we live in—you're brought up to think it's wrong to kill, then have to go to the army to be trained to kill.

BOY: I don't worry about it—I just put my mind in
                neutral and don't think.

BOY: I sometimes wonder how much relieved everybody
                would be if we knew there wouldn't be another
                war. It's something that's sort of curled up in your
                mind, like a snake—you walk around it, but it's al-
                ways there, waiting, waiting.

C: It's hard to be yourself. It's hard to know where
                you stand, and what you stand for.

L: I get the feeling sometimes that I'm surrounded.
                People come at me from all directions with sug-
                gestions, orders, ideas, pressures.

C: (*diminishing in volume with each repetition*) It's
                hard to be yourself. It's hard to be yourself. It's
                hard. It's hard.

Interpreting Bible Study

Although the new translations of the Bible make it more
understandable to children and young people, it is helpful, occasionally, in studying the Bible to have groups make their own
modern "translations" of particular verses or groups of verses.
Junior-high and senior-high young people, once they find it possible to drop clichés, can penetrate perceptively into the meaning
of a Bible passage as they "translate" it into their own language.
One boy wrote the following terse paraphrase of Jesus' response to the would-be followers (Luke 9:57-62) who wanted to
put something else ahead of the Kingdom: "Quit stalling! Don't
give me any more high-sounding excuses! Either you want to do
this now, or you want to do something else. Make up your minds.
You can't have it both ways." The radical demands of Jesus make
themselves felt in this unorthodox interpretation of Jesus' words.
Writing a meditation on a particular passage is another way
of breaking open the meaning of the Bible. The attempt is made
to personalize what is being said, to see as honestly as possible
what this means for our lives. A teacher wrote the following

meditation on Matthew 5:43-48 (the demand of Jesus that we love our enemies):

> I am asked to forget the grudges, peeves, and slights I have nursed along. Anybody can love someone who is lovable and who loves him in turn; but I am asked to speak to people who ignore me or turn away from me; to care about people who don't care about me; to think about whether a person needs my concern, rather than whether he deserves it; to respond positively to people who respond negatively to me. Only in this way can I participate in God's dealing with people. He looks at what is needed, acts accordingly, and loves accordingly. It isn't easy, judging myself by such a standard, to be good in God's eyes. It demands all-inclusive or perfect love.

A most fruitful discussion can follow the making of such paraphrases and meditations, as each person reads his own writing and the group talks about the meaning of the passage.

Writing a Psalm

Children need familiarity with several Psalms before they can be expected to create one of their own. The group should experiment with expressing ideas in rhythmic and repetitive patterns such as occur in many of the Psalms. In choosing Psalms to use as patterns, care should be exercised to find those that do not include vindictive statements about destruction of enemies and that do not portray God as an arbitrary, wrathful Being. A few verses from a Psalm, especially with younger children, may be sufficient. Psalms 23, 24, 100, 103, 121, and 122 are a few of the more familiar ones.

Writing a psalm may grow out of some especially happy time the group has had together. Since many of the Psalms express deep depression and discouragement, a group might very well look at some of these at a time when things are not going well in the group, and then attempt to formulate their own ideas in the form of a psalm.

Several classes have selected familiar hymn tunes and have written psalms to fit the music.

Writing a Summary Statement

There are many ways to sum up a unit of study in creative writing. One way is to write a one-sentence capsule of the "big idea" of each session. These capsules can be written on the chalkboard and sometimes can be used as a choral reading. The teacher may serve as narrator and intersperse little comments and details about each event and person.

A junior group prepared a prose poem summarizing a unit of study. They worked it out during the several weeks spent on the unit, then used it with one member reading, "We wondered . . . ," another reading, "We learned . . . ," and the group together reading all the responses. A part of the poem follows:

WE WONDERED AND LEARNED

We wondered . . .
    Who made God?
We learned . . .
    That God was even before
    he planned and created
    the world.
We wondered . . .
    Who is God?
We learned . . .
    That God is not a man
    But a Spirit of Love
    Who is in all people,
    Wanting us to live
    His good way.
We wondered . . .
    Where is God?
We learned . . .
    God is not in one place

But everywhere;
With us all the time.
We wondered . . .
    If God is a Spirit, how
    can he help us?
We learned . . .
    As we think quietly about
    God he puts thoughts
    into our minds;
    When we ask God in prayer
    He will help us.

. . . .

We wondered . . .
    What is God's plan for
    people?
We learned . . .
    God planned for people,
    His greatest creation,
    To love God,
    Who is like a loving father;
    God planned for people
    To discover the secrets
    He put into the universe
    And to use them for the
    good of all;
    God planned for people
    To live his laws of love
    And helpfulness
    As Jesus did;
    God planned for people
    To work with him
    To help others know
    God better;
    To make our world good
    As he planned it to be;
    "He can use my hand!"[1]

[1] Written by fourth-grade boys and girls in Hudson, Ohio. From "They Wondered and Learned," by Florence Cronon. Reprinted from *Children's Religion*, March 1952, copyright 1952, The Pilgrim Press.

BIBLIOGRAPHY

Brown, Helen, *Choral Reading for Worship and Inspiration.* Philadelphia: The Westminster Press, 1954.

————, *Let's Read Together Poems.* Evanston: Harper & Row, Publishers, 1949.

Gullan, Marjorie, *Choral Speaking.* London: Methuen, 1957.

DeBanke, Cecile, *The Art of Choral Speaking.* Boston: Bakers' Plays, 1937.

Hamm, Agnes C., *Choral Speaking Technique.* Milwaukee: The Tower Press, 1946.

XIII

Ways to Make Discussion Fruitful

In several of the preceding chapters, examples of discussion have been given. A high school group studying Amos started with an opinion poll. Fifth- and sixth-graders discussed among themselves the question "Who is God?" Third- and fourth-graders tried to decide whether Joseph was a spoiled child. In each case there was possible a divergence of points of view, and this factor stimulated discussion.

Not all two-way conversation is discussion. The most fruitful discussion centers around a problem to which a group is seeking an answer or solution. Discussion is not a question-and-answer situation in which the teacher probes for the "right" answer nor one in which he gives a lecture, with opportunity for questions. Real discussion comes only if there is a problem or controversy about which the group can talk. If a group needs to find the one "right" answer to a question, discussion is not needed, but rather some means of stimulating the group to find that answer through study, research, or question and answer.

True discussion is an attempt to discover and evaluate alternative solutions to a problem. The teacher, because of his experience and maturity, may know what are some of the solutions, but his aim is to help the group think constructively to formulate them. He may suggest a possibility now and then, but should be careful in doing so not to let the students think that there is a right answer that they must attempt to guess. Essentially, discussion is group thinking and problem-solving.

The emphasis in discussion is not on imparting knowledge, but on stimulating children or young people to wrestle intellectually with a problem. This is not to say that there is no place for the presentation of information. There is! Yet there is also the need to grapple with matters in which there are many possible answers and solutions. In fact, the same material may be approached through both presentation and discussion. For example, in learning about the last week of Jesus' life, the students will need to have clearly in mind what actually happened. To help them recall these facts, the teacher may, therefore, ask certain questions:

What do we know about the last week of Jesus' life?

Why did some of the scribes and Pharisees dislike Jesus?

According to the Gospels, what happened each day of the last week?

By referring to their textbooks, to the Bible, and to resource books, the class can determine the answers to these and other questions. The students may talk them over among themselves to check for accuracy.

If the teacher then wishes to add a dimension of creative thinking through discussion, he can raise such questions as the following:

Is there anything worth dying for?

If you had been in Jesus' place, what other ways than dying might you have chosen to accomplish your purpose?

What can you do when people turn against you or accuse you unjustly?

These questions do not have "right" answers—at least, answers that are immediately apparent. They require a group to look at various alternatives and choose the one that seems most appropriate. They call for creative thinking and problem-solving. It may be that one reason for discipline problems in some classes is that the discussion is not real; nothing more is expected from the participants than that they discover the answer which the teacher knew all the time. Wonder and searching for answers to penetrating questions seem out of place in such a setting.

The discussion procedures described below are only a few of the many possible approaches. They may help a teacher to work out other means of stimulating creative thought about important matters.

Small Groups Discuss and Report Back

Even a class of ten or twelve is sometimes too large for participation and involvement of all members. Breaking up the class into units of four or five persons, each with a student leader, often can help a class to be productive. Each small group discusses the problematic question before it, which offers several possible conclusions, and reaches a decision about the recommendation it will make, with one of its members reporting back to the class. Out of all the reports will emerge discussion by the large group.

Pro and Con Discussion

This method is somewhat arbitrary and artificial, but it is useful in helping students think through a position different from that which they might ordinarily take. The group is divided, one part to take the "pro" position about a question, no matter how the individual members feel personally, and the other half to take the "con" position.

The teacher states a question weighted in favor of neither side but which has strong possibilities on both sides. Representatives from the two sides speak alternately, after some time has been given for members of each group to consult among themselves. The teacher writes on the chalkboard the points made by each side.

A variation of this method for use with high-school young people is to have them write down ahead of time their individual points of view. They then participate in the pro and con discussion, and afterward write down again what they feel individually is the best solution to the problem. It is interesting to see whether the discussion has produced any shifts in position or has only solidified the original points of view.

Opinion Poll, True-False Questionnaire

These are variations of one technique. A list of statements or questions is prepared that, in so far as possible, are open to two or more answers. The teacher makes clear that there is no "right" answer—that each individual must try to decide where he should stand in relation to the question and should answer accordingly. After each person has checked or indicated his response, the teacher goes over the list again and asks what opinions were indicated. If it is a true-false list, he asks which persons marked the answer to a question as "true" and which marked it "false." He then asks those taking each position to defend their answer, giving their reasons for thinking as they do. If the subject is one of genuine interest to the group, it is almost impossible to keep discussion from flowing at this point.

Courtroom Scene

The class is divided into three parts: the prosecution, the defense, and the judge or jury. A person whom the class has studied is "put on trial." For example, the father of the prodigal son might be tried for contributing to and supporting delinquency. The prosecution points out reasons why the father's actions might contribute to delinquency. The defense thinks up reasons why his actions were right and did not contribute to the son's delinquency. The judge or jury decides which group has presented the best evidence and passes sentence or frees the accused. Discussion takes place during the preparation, the presentation of arguments, and after the decision.

The purpose of having such a trial is not to sharpen debating skills but to give participants an opportunity to think deeply about the story. Jesus told the story to show that God is like the father who extended unconditional love to his son. Many people, not understanding this, think that yielding to the whims of his son and then receiving him back after he had squandered the money only invited recklessness. Yet it was the unconditional nature of the father's love that made it like God's love.

This procedure can also be used, of course, to probe the meaning of other stories and events.

Preference Sort

This procedure, which is described in Chapter XI, can be used as a discussion stimulator. It consists of sorting alternative solutions for a problem into categories according to favorable, unfavorable, and neutral responses to them. After the sorting, members of a class discuss the alternative solutions.

For example, after a study of the life of Jesus or of some situation in the church or community, the group might like to discuss the question, "How do we tell right from wrong?" The teacher may list on slips of paper many ways, ranging from the most acceptable by Christian standards to the least acceptable (but nevertheless practiced) ways. The first and last piles might be limited to not more than three slips. This causes the members to do some careful thinking to eliminate the slips that do not belong in those piles. A vigorous discussion is likely to follow the sorting.

Some groups use the preference sort more than one time, the teacher recording the numbers of each member one Sunday and then comparing the numbers placed in the piles in the sort the next Sunday. The students can then discuss the reasons why they made or did not make changes in the positions of the various slips.

In another variation, students circle on a sheet of paper five words, out of a field of twenty or twenty-five, that they believe most adequately characterize a person in the study unit, or the best of a number of solutions to a problem. This may be done individually or in small groups. The teacher then writes on the board the five words each member or small group has chosen, and the larger group discusses them.

In another variation, members of a group indicate their preferences of pictures in a selection. Which of a certain selection best represents Jesus? Which in another selection best represents what a ten-year-old (or other age) boy ought to be? In another group, which picture best represents a mother or father? (See "Pictures with Which to Identify" and "Preference Sort" in Chapter XI.)

Role-Playing

Older juniors, young people, and adults have found role-playing helpful in getting deeply into the heart of a problem and discussing it. Two, three, or more persons assume the roles of persons in some specific situation, try to see things as those persons would, and react as they would in the situation. There may be no specific plot, beginning, or climax to role-playing, and the teacher will probably cut off the playing when the participants have had opportunity to understand the issues involved and have responded meaningfully to each other in their roles.

Ordinary experiences of life are the material for role-playing. For example, a junior-high boy's conflict with his family over his curfew may be the "story." The group gives each member of the family certain characteristics: the father is arbitrary and auto-cratic; the mother is permissive and indulgent; the boy is concerned with how other young people look at him and he wants to be one of the crowd. The persons portraying the roles must try to express, not their own feelings, but those of the persons they are portraying. The dialogue is not planned, as this is, in effect, playing from life. Each person responds to what is said or done to him in the situation, rather than in the way he might have decided in advance to respond.

The most important part of the process is the evaluation following the role-playing. The cast and other members of the class decide whether each member of the cast played the role to which he was assigned and how the action affected the rest of the cast. Questions such as these may be directed to the members of the cast: Did you feel differently toward your father when you finished than when you started? Did you feel that he understood what you were trying to say? Do you feel that it would be easier to work out a problem with him another time? How could you change so that the situation would be one of greater understanding?

The value of the role-playing is not so much in solving problems as in helping young people and adults to see the way another person feels and to grasp the interdependence of persons in working out an understanding. Role-playing gives a person practice in putting into words how he would feel in a given situation, rather than theorizing about what he ought to do or say. This kind of penetrating experience opens up a problem for meaningful discussion.

These and other procedures can help a group think creatively in its discussions, rather than simply air superficial opinions and prejudices.

XIV

Use of Resource
Persons, Interviews,
and Trips

Many youth groups and church school classes have found in trips and visits with resource persons the means of gathering information, understanding problems, and broadening their horizons in a most interesting way.

The Use of Visiting Resource Persons

The work of a class may be greatly enriched by visits of resource persons who can share certain interests with the group. As with all teaching procedures, the use of visitors, to be most fruitful, must be for a specific purpose and be part of a planned program of study. The interest or information shared should be related to what the group has been doing or is about to undertake, or to some matter of long-range interest such as missionary outreach.

It is important that the group participate in making arrangements, in preparation for the visit, and in follow-up. The group can compose a letter of invitation; or, in the case of older chil-

193

KINDS OF RESOURCE PERSONS CONTRIBUTING
TO VARIOUS GROUPS

Age Group	Resource Person	Unit of Study
All age groups.	The minister. The sexton. Members of official boards. The choir director or organist.	On the local church.
Nursery and kindergarten.	A doctor. A postman. A fireman. A farmer.	Helpers in the community.
Junior, junior high, senior high.	A person who has lived in the Holy Land. A person who has visited the Holy Land. A local Jewish family, to show and tell about the mezuzah and Jewish Holy Days. A rabbi, to tell about the significance of the Passover in the Bible. A teacher or artist who can show samples of illuminated writing such as was used in copying the Bible before printing. A person to sing Palestinian folk songs or Hebrew hymns and Psalms.	The Bible lands, the Old Testament, the Life of Jesus, or the story of the Bible.
Junior high, senior high.	A person from another denomination to interpret the story and the distinctiveness of his group. An architect, artist, or traveler to talk about church buildings through the centuries. A missionary to tell of the work of the church in another part of the world. A native Christian from another country to tell of the work of his church. A member of the choir to sing and talk about some kind of church music: early chants, anthems and oratorios, Psalms, and hymns.	The story of the church.

dren, a committee can extend the invitation by telephone or in person. In advance of the visit, the class can decide what they want to find out from the visitor and can make a list of questions to be asked. Following the visit, they will thank the visitor by letter and will decide how they can use what they learned in further study.

Because of the variety of subject matter, it is impossible to indicate all the opportunities, but on page 194 is a list of some of the kinds of resource persons that have contributed to various groups. Ways in which each is used varies with the unit of study and the age of the students.

The Use of Interviews

Sometimes it is better for a class or part of a class to go to see a resource person, rather than ask him to come to the class. A very busy person may prefer to chat for a few minutes with a committee rather than come to the class for a longer time. In some cases the resource person is not available at the time the class meets (because of other commitments and responsibilities). It may be that only part of the class needs certain information and can secure it through an interview. There are advantages in the interview approach: the group must take the initiative rather than rely on the resource person to come to them; the interviewers do the traveling, ask the questions, and report back to the larger group. The first-hand involvement of the members of the committee requires that they plan before the interview and evaluate afterward. The teacher will guide the group in phrasing questions so that they are neither blunt nor politely meaningless.

The Use of Trips

Trips by classes or departmental groups may have various purposes. A trip may be taken to enable the members of a group to become better acquainted with each other: a picnic or barbecue at the home of a member; a hike through the woods in the spring or fall. A trip may be taken for worship in a sunrise service, a quiet time in a forest, or a vesper service by a river or lake. It may be taken to gather information or do research: a visit to a Catholic church, a Greek Orthodox church, a Jewish synagogue, a church of another denomination, the home of a Jewish family at the time of the Feast of the Booths (harvest time), a museum, or an exhibit that is relevant to the study which the group is carrying on. A trip may be taken to stimulate interest in a unit of study or a giving project: a study tour of a blighted housing area, of migrant working conditions, an orphanage, or a community center (appropriate for junior children and young people who can do something about what they see). A trip may be in the nature of a day camp for juniors, a week-end retreat for junior-high or senior-high young people, or an extended session held in a different setting.

For young children, a trip may be as simple as a walk around the block to see the flowers coming in the spring, to listen to birds, or to watch the snow. Children as young as kindergarten and primary can sing Christmas carols to shut-ins. High-school young people may make a trip of three to six weeks, studying and working in some place where there is great social need which they can meet, contributing their talents and learning from the people they serve.

In order to make good use of resource people, interviews, and trips, a teacher needs to be acquainted with his community. He needs to know who are the people with special information needed by the class, and he needs to discover the places to which a class trip can be fruitful for the class members.

XV

Creative Activities for Preschool Children

In teaching preschool children, an important aim is to help them to become trusting, loving persons. Some of the many facets of this task are mentioned in Chapter V, and the following suggestions are intended to supplement those given in that chapter.

Every child needs the experience of being a worthful human being, capable, adequate, and competent in doing things which he holds to be important. As he has this experience, he tends to become less self-protective and more able to be concerned with other persons. Self-respect precedes and underlies respect for others.

Among the most important learnings that go on in the preschool years are those that occur in the associations of child with child and child with adult. Learning to trust oneself and others, learning to give and receive, learning to venture into friendship, learning to remedy mistakes—all of these are among the important Christian foundations to be developed during the preschool years. In the attempt to have children learn something specific each Sunday, we must be careful not to undercut these basic, long-range experiences. For example, the teacher may want children to learn that the church is a friendly place. He will bear in mind that a friendly atmosphere will help them learn it better than any number of activities about churches. A group of children playing happily in the block corner learn in a deep and long-lasting way that the church is a friendly place. No words are necessary, for this kind of learning requires no words. No churches of blocks need to be built, for a picture of the church as a friendly place is being built into the lives of the children. A shy child painting an apparently random picture at the easel for the first time is learning that the church is a place where grown-ups trust him to do things he has never done before, where he is important to grown-ups. This is a much more important learning than what might come through pasting a colored church (cut out by the teacher) on a piece of paper.

The use of free and creative activities in church school often raises questions in the minds of parents and teachers. "Is this free activity teaching the children anything about Christianity?" they often ask. To understand the contribution which free activities can make to a child's experience, it is necessary to remember that one of the long-range goals of teaching preschool children is to help them become loving and trusting persons. If the children are only talked to, or participate only in activities directed by the teacher, it is difficult for the teacher to know at what points each child is or is not growing in his ability to understand, trust, and love others. It is in the spontaneous interactions of children that a listening, sensitive teacher can find out what progress is being made by a child in living religiously with others. As a child relates naturally to other children, a teacher is able to see him as he is (rather than as he would like him to be) and is thereby able to deal with the day-to-day matters that keep him from becoming a loving person.

Since a child is able to trust others only as he learns to trust himself, we must evaluate each procedure used by asking, "Does it add to his sense that 'I can do it'?" Pattern activities, for example, in which the work is done by the teacher, or planned by him in such a way as to limit the freedom of the child, do not meet that test. Although the product may be attractive (at least, to the teacher) and may "fit the lesson," it is doubtful whether it increases the child's trust in himself. Any activity that tends to put the emphasis on producing a specific thing is questionable for preschool children, who lack the ability to reproduce an object in clay, paint, or other materials.

If the children sense that what is wanted is a specific object, they often ask the teacher to "make me a church (or house, or tree)." If, on the other hand, they are free to experiment and use materials in their own way, they become engrossed for surprisingly long periods of time without appeals for help.

How quickly a group of four-years-olds patting, pounding, and rolling clay is changed by the appearance of a teacher who sits down and begins to make something. All eyes become focused on the teacher's handiwork. Each child knows that he cannot do what the teacher has done and is likely to say, "Make me one, too." The children's "I can do it" feeling has been stifled rather than encouraged.

Children should be offered activities within their physical capabilities. Few three-year-olds can manage scissors well, and even fewer have the muscular coordination to stay within prescribed lines when coloring. Young children are frustrated and irritated by activities that call for fine coordination of eyes and hands, because they cannot enter into them without help from an adult. The fine-muscle abilities are not yet developed. Most children are of kindergarten age and older before they begin to draw or paint anything representational—that is, recognizable as a house, person, or tree. They draw and paint with great enjoyment prior to that time if given the opportunity, labeling the picture, if at all, after it is finished. The sheer joy of creating is satisfaction enough, and it is not necessary to "make something."

Many preschool activities, therefore, do not teach any specific "lesson." They contribute to the child's ability to express his feelings, to experiment, to create, and to try new experiences. These are important ingredients of the religious life, which is essentially a life of trust and faith, of venturing into new experiences and associations in which one simply "goes out in faith." As young children learn to create something at their own level of ability, they take part in the remarkable process of creating and re-creating that is continually a part of our lives and is undergirded by the Creator himself.

The activities described below are suggested for three-, four-, and five-years-olds. A few may be useful with two-year-olds.

EXPERIMENTING WITH MATERIALS

The use of new materials in molding, pasting, assembling, and painting can open to young children a new world of wonderment and creativity.

Play Dough or Clay

Children from two to five years of age enjoy manipulating clay or dough (hereafter referred to as *clay*). Children from three to five enjoy mixing the clay prior to playing with it. The teacher provides measuring cups, a pitcher of water, flour, salt, a large mixing bowl (unbreakable), and large spoons. Two parts of flour to one part of salt are gradually moistened with water to which vegetable color has been added. If the clay becomes too sticky, more flour is added; if too crumbly, more water is added. Each child has a turn at stirring the mixture. When it is finally ready, each is given a lump of clay. A little pile of flour for each child keeps the fresh clay from sticking to hands and table. When the session is over, the clay may be stored in a closed container and kept for several weeks if refrigerated.

A shy child can safely venture to the clay table because he can play with his own clay without having to make conversation with anyone. The vigorous child can pat and pound as much as he desires. Sociable children can compare balls and swap bits of clay. The malleable, changing form of clay is intriguing and satisfying to all children.

Pasting

Pasting offers some of the same satisfactions as working in clay, with the advantage that one can make a "picture" to take home. Children like the cool, sticky feeling of paste between their fingers, and enjoy using it to make pictures, or collages. Sheets of manila paper, newsprint, or colored paper are used as background. The material to be pasted on the sheets can vary greatly: random pieces of colored construction paper, shaped pieces (circles, triangles, rectangles), bits of yarn, ribbon, lace, or cloth, pieces of wallpaper, buttons, seeds, sections of drinking straws, and grass. Making a collage by pasting many items in original shapes and combinations is a favorite activity.

Stringing

Some two-year-olds can string large beads on a heavy string. Many three-, four-, and five-year-olds enjoy making necklaces, decorating a Christmas tree, and fixing strings of food for birds in wintertime. Cranberries, Cheerios, pieces of macaroni, and large wooden beads are some of the materials that can be strung together. The needles should be blunt-pointed with big eyes.

Painting

Making a picture at an easel, with a painting smock to protect Sunday clothes, is often a new experience for preschoolers. They may have used tempera paints at home, but few have easels and assorted colors. Large sheets of paper (18" x 24" or larger) are attached with clips to the top of the easel. A four-legged easel is preferable to the tripod variety because it is steadier, and there can be a board on each side so that two children can paint at the same time. A brush (long-handled and full-bristled) is provided for each color of paint, so that no washing of brushes is necessary while in use. Sometimes a child likes to have the teacher write a "story" on his painting as he tells her what it is all about. The emphasis, however, is on the enjoyable creation of something new, not on producing something that can be labeled.

Churches that do not have easels can provide painting experiences by putting pads of newspaper on the floor and placing paint cans or jars in tin cans that have been nailed to a wide board to avoid spilling the paint. Sheets of plain newsprint are then placed on the pads for the children to use in painting. Smocks made from old shirts will protect their clothing as the children kneel to paint.

Finger Painting

This is an activity that involves experimenting with color, texture, and movement, and allows for expression of feelings and the relaxation of tension. Glazed shelf paper or commercial finger-paint paper is provided for each child who wants to finger paint. The paper is dipped into a pan of water, then is spread on a table with several sheets of newspaper under it if the table needs protection. A blob of finger paint is placed on the paper. The child uses his fingers, hands, and forearms to spread the paint over the paper in constantly changing patterns and designs. Music in the background is enjoyable and helps to create a mood for the painting.

If the tables are smooth and easily washed, children can finger paint directly on them. A child does not have something to take home, but he has experienced the free movement and relaxation without the necessity of producing a final design and waiting for the picture to dry so that it can be taken home.

Finger painting with soapsuds on oilcloth or table top is similar to the activities just described. Soap flakes are beaten with a small amount of water until light and fluffy. Food coloring may be added if desired. The slippery, soft feeling and the fact that the soap is easily washed off make this a practical and interesting activity.

In warm climates and in vacation schools, water painting is enjoyable. Tubs of water are provided outdoors, with wide paint brushes. The children "paint" the sidewalk, trees, stones and fence with water. This activity is relaxing to some children and gives others a sense of "doing something like Daddy does."

Stamping or Sponge Painting

Older four-year-olds and five-year-olds enjoy painting with small sponges, spools, orange-juice cans, spice cans, and other articles, which they dip into tempera paint and then stamp on paper. For example, an orange-juice can makes a circle design. This activity is not recommended for two-, three-, and younger four-year-olds because it requires some coordination.

Drawing with Crayons and Chalk

Large pieces of paper, usually placed on tables, are necessary because preschool children use large arm movements in drawing with crayons or chalk. It is best to use thick crayons or chalk that does not break easily under pressure. White paper with colored crayon or chalk ordinarily is used, but dark paper (blue or black) and white chalk are good for winter activity. Snow pictures, star pictures, and many other varieties come into being at the hands of the "artists." To reduce the powdering of chalk, the paper can be dipped in water, or bowls of water can be provided so that the chalk may be dipped.

CARING FOR GROWING THINGS

Preschool children need experience in caring for plants and animals. They need to observe the growth of a seed from sprout to leaf to flower to seed. They need to ask questions, to wonder, and to listen. They need to think about what we can do and cannot do to assist growth. They need to have the experience of handling and caring for animals that are smaller and more helpless than they are. Gentleness and tenderness are observed as they see teachers handle baby kittens or guinea pigs. They then learn to be gentle as they handle the animals inquiringly.

Young children, especially three-year-olds, need to see immediate results from planting seeds. Beans or radishes are probably the most satisfactory, because they sprout rapidly.

Sweet potatoes, carrots, and beets, when sliced and placed in water, often sprout new tops. Green plants in the room that need watering give children the sense that they can do something important. Caring for and feeding fish, turtles, hamsters, and guinea pigs give children an essential experience of being responsible for living things.

Occasionally a litter of puppies or kittens, or a parakeet, may be brought to the room. Even a new baby may be brought to visit the group after the children have learned how important it is to be gentle and quiet when dealing with young and helpless creatures.

CREATING THROUGH IMAGINATIVE PLAY

Play is the business of small children. Through play they find out about their world and how to relate to other persons. In play they express their feelings and ideas. In play they try on what it is like to be another person.

Both boys and girls enjoy playing house, caring for babies, washing dishes, dressing up to go to the store, and in other ways trying on what it is like to be an adult. For this reason it is important to have a housekeeping center in the room, with dress-up clothes. In dealing with the dolls and with each other, children put into words their feelings about themselves and others: "This dolly is always bad. She never can do anything right. She will have to be punished. I'll hit her hard." What is this child saying about himself in talking about the doll?

Playing with blocks, preferably large ones, offers many possibilities for imaginative and dramatic play, and for older four-year-olds and five-year-olds to begin to learn how to work together in building things.

Imaginative play is not an activity that teachers can plan ahead of time, except by providing the materials with which it can occur. The teacher's role is that of listening rather than of initiating. Only in this way can the teacher begin to enter the world of the child, discovering how he looks at himself and other people. Until the teacher has this first-hand information, gleaned by quiet listening, it is difficult for him to determine whether the stories and other activities are helpful and appropriate.

Chapter XVII gives several examples of preschool drama activities. Formal dramatization is not appropriate for young children, but spontaneous physical response to songs, stories, and pictures is quite appropriate. Small children often react to music by swaying, clapping, or moving. With a suggestion from the teacher, they put themselves whole-heartedly into being a whirling snowflake, a falling autumn leaf, a hopping bunny, a squirrel busily gathering nuts. They like to play-act that they are firemen, policemen, milkmen, mommy, daddy, and many other familiar characters.

HAVING NEW EXPERIENCES

Many of the activities described may be new to some preschool children; other activities will be new to all of the children. New activities as well as familiar ones hold possibilities of wonderment and the experience of creativity. One preschool vacation-school group churned its own butter one day, then each child had a little of it to work with and taste, while squeezing out the water and milk. The next day a teacher brought bread dough already mixed, and each child kneaded and patted a little loaf, putting it aside to rise, then taking it to the church kitchen for baking. Afterward each spread his butter on his bread, ate part of it, then took the rest home as a gift to his family. Simple activities such as making instant pudding for a special treat, baking cookies, or making apple sauce provide many opportunities for conversation about how people work together to have food, and how dependent we are on God's plan for seasons and growth.

A trip to see baby lambs in the spring or to visit a chicken farm is a new experience for most preschoolers and offers many opportunities for conversation about the wonderful process of growth.

These suggestions indicate the many possibilities for young children to have experiences that will widen their understanding of the world, of God's activity, and of their dependence on other people. All activities used with preschool children should help them grow in a sense of adequacy and worthfulness, in the ability increasingly to take responsibility for their own actions as these affect themselves and other people, and in a continuing sense of wonder and awe.

XVI

The Use of Construction Activities with Children

The activities mentioned in this section involve the use and manipulation of various materials. As with all other activities mentioned in the book, their use is determined by the content of the study that the group is making, the interests of the children, and the length of time available.

Whenever possible, it is best to have in mind two or three alternative construction activities that might provide interesting approaches to learning in a particular unit of study. The children may have finished making a mural in school recently but would be interested in a diorama, for example. Freedom to choose among alternatives is an important part of the learning process.

The teacher does not need to be artistic, nor even able to draw, in order to use construction activities with children. Occasionally a teacher with exceptional artistic ability finds it harder than a person without such talent, because he has such high expectations of the children and envisions more beautiful and perfect things than the children can create. Enthusiasm and encouragement are the most important qualities of the teacher. The children, with some stimulation through questions and suggestions, will do the work, provided they feel that their efforts are acceptable to the teacher. When the teacher does the work, the results may be more beautiful, but the children do not have the satisfaction or learning that comes from having to work things out for themselves. Any activity that requires considerable help from the teacher should be omitted. This is true even with three- and four-year-olds. If the teacher succumbs to the temptation to do part of the work or make a pattern to be copied, the children become disinterested because they cannot duplicate the teacher's work.

There are children who actively dislike doing anything with their hands. The teacher should not force them against their will, but try to discover the reason for their reluctance. Some children simply lack confidence in their ability to do things with their hands. At this point a non-artistic teacher can sometimes be of most help, demonstrating that even he has trouble carrying out what he visualizes, but that perfection is not the goal. Encouragement and praise often buttress a child enough so that he can venture into a simple effort at first, to be followed by a bigger one later. If a child is adamant consistently and does not respond to encouragement, other activities, relating to the class project, should be found for him. He might do research work; he might find and mount pictures that help the children who are working on the activity; or he might be the narrator or the supply chairman.

Construction activity is not an end in itself. It is used to clarify and elaborate the learning that is going on in other ways. The interest span of children should be reckoned with carefully, so that activities are proposed that do not require so much time that the children will lose interest. Often there are mechanical preparations that can be done at home by individuals or committees or in an extra session of the class.

Before work is begun, the teacher should be sure that the

group is well informed about the subject matter to which the activities are related. He should have on hand books, maps, pictures, and other materials that will help the children become acquainted with the geography, historical background, and customs represented in the event to be portrayed.

The activities described are only a few of those found useful. The suggestions are given as a stimulus to teachers and may help them find other activities that are interesting and full of learning possibilities.

Diorama

A diorama is like a miniature stage setting. Children may have seen good examples of large (often life-size) dioramas in museums of natural history, where stuffed animals are displayed in natural habitat.

A cardboard box can be used as the "stage," the top being cut off and the box turned on its side. The background scenery for the diorama is painted or drawn on construction paper fitted around the three sides of the box. It is often effective to have the scenery paper curved around the back of the stage rather than fitted into the corners. Older children can take a trip to a museum to see the way in which perspective is created. Younger children will not need to try to represent perspective. When older children want to have a receding effect in the background, it is helpful to place an object on the stage, such as a tree, then have objects similar in shape and color but in diminishing sizes repeated on the construction-paper background.

Figures of persons for the foreground are made from clothespins, clay, and pipestem cleaners, or from cardboard, and are dressed and placed in the scene. Trees, houses, rocks, boats, and other objects are modeled from clay or cut from cardboard. The teacher will help children to put in enough detail so that the story or event portrayed can be understood by looking at the diorama.

Box Movie

In simplest form, a box movie is a series of pictures on a roll of paper, the ends of which are attached to dowel rods mounted in a cardboard box in such a way that one rod can be turned, pulling the pictures off the other rod past the opening to become the "motion picture."

The roll of paper is laid out on the tops of two or three tables, end-to-end. Squares are outlined lightly with pencil, with a border one and one-half inches to two inches at top and bottom, and that much or a little more space between squares. In each of the squares, a member of the group draws and colors a picture representing some person, event, or scene in the unit of study. If there is not room to spread the roll, individual pictures can be made in class or at home, then pasted on the roll. Titles can be added to the pictures.

The cardboard box should be larger than the width of the roll of paper. A hole large enough to accommodate the pictures is cut in the side facing the "audience," with the border of cardboard forming a frame for the pictures.

Most groups cut a hole in the top of the box at each side and insert the rods vertically so that the pictures move horizontally. A tack through the bottom of the box into each dowel rod will hold the rod in place. The tack head should be covered with a piece of cardboard to protect the table. Because the roll droops when this is done, some groups prefer to put the rods in horizontally, one across the top and one across the bottom, so that the picture roll moves vertically. Then the pictures need to be made individually and pasted on the roll. The "crank" to turn the roll can be made of a piece of heavy wire, with one end wrapped around an end of one rod. Another crank, attached to the other rod, can be used to reverse the roll.

This activity is especially useful for summary or review at the end of a unit. At that time there will have been a number of stories, people, or events discussed, so that each child can choose a portion that he would like to represent.

Mural

A church school mural may be painted directly on a wall but usually is painted on a large sheet of paper or cloth to be hung on a wall. A class may be divided into committees to work on different sections of the mural: one for the background, one for the buildings, and another for the people. After preliminary planning in the whole group, members of each committee talk together and make pencil sketches of their part. Then they meet with the other committees to compare ideas. The whole mural is sketched in chalk on the wall, paper, or cloth before painting is started.

An alternative method is to have each committee paint its part on a separate sheet of paper, which is then cut out around the actual painting and pasted on the mural paper. This method has the advantage of making it possible for some children to do additional work at home or at the church between sessions without holding up the entire group. Also, the scenery or background committee can work directly on the mural paper while other groups are working elsewhere on separate sheets, thus avoiding congestion around the mural.

A class should paint directly on the wall only if the group is sufficiently interested to do the work carefully and well. (The wall can be washed or repainted.) In contrast with a paper mural, a wall painting is "real." Older juniors and junior highs may be enthusiastic about painting on the wall, but think that making a paper mural is "kid stuff."

Frieze

A frieze also is placed on a wall or on a wall tack board, but is composed of a sequence or series of pictures. Each child selects the part of the study that he would like to portray. The picture he makes (with or without a caption, as the group desires) is pasted on a long band of paper to be placed on the wall.

Another way to prepare a frieze is to place a long strip of paper, divided into sections, on some tables or on the floor. The teacher explains that on it they will represent the unit of study just completed, each section portraying a story or event. The class decides what caption would be appropriate in each section, and a child is assigned to portray the story or event represented. When completed, the strip is placed on the wall or tackboard.

A variation is to have the teacher whisper to each child the name of the section he is to make, so that when he has finished the rest of the group can try to guess which section he has portrayed.

A frieze may be made as a one-day review or as a long-term project.

Lantern Slides

Juniors and junior highs enjoy creating pictures that can be projected. Projection adds enchantment and interest to the undertaking. Frosted glass and colored pencils are used in making lantern slides. Frosted glass is available at photographic shops or can be made by rubbing Carborundum powder between two pieces of clear glass. The glass should be 3¼″ x 4″ if a projector for that size slide is available. Or if it is not available, the slides can be placed on white paper and used in an opaque projector.

The class discusses the unit of study and decides which parts they would like to represent in the slide set. Each child chooses the part he wishes to draw.

The picture is sketched first on a piece of paper. To outline the area for the picture, the child places the glass on a sheet of paper and draws a pencil line around the glass. Removing the glass, he draws another line about ⅜ inch in from each side of the rectangle, to form a border around the picture. He draws his picture within the smaller rectangle.

The glass is then placed, frosted side up, on top of the picture. The child then colors the picture with colored pencils. The coloring should be heavy enough so that it will be vivid when the picture is projected on the screen. The coloring must be evenly applied. A painted effect can be given by going over the colors lightly with a wet brush.

When the picture is completed and has dried, it can be covered with a piece of clear glass the same size and the two pieces bound together with tape made for binding slides or with masking tape.

An interesting correlated activity can be the writing of a script to go with the slide set. Some groups enjoy tape-recording the story so that they have a set of "sound" slides.

Acetate Transparencies

Many groups prefer to make larger transparencies from frosted acetate. This offers the advantage that the transparencies are easier to work with and are less fragile than glass. An illuminated viewer can be made for showing them. The acetate is available by the yard from many art supply stores. It can be cut with scissors to the desired size (perhaps 8″ x 8″) and mounted on frames made of ½″ x ¼″ wood strips. On the frosted side, pictures can be drawn or painted with colored pencils, wax crayons, ink, or paint.

Several kinds of viewers have been made for showing the large slides. A simple one can be made by cutting a hole the size of the transparencies in the side of a cardboard box and mounting a slide track with a flange on it below the hole and one above to hold the transparency in place as it slides in front of the hole. The box is then lined with glazed white paper to serve as a reflector. An electric extension cord is dropped through a hole in the top of the box, several inches from the reflector, and a light bulb put in it (the reflector should be at least 18 to 24 inches from the transparency). The group can experiment with curving the reflector inside the box to provide even distribution of light on the transparency.

Usually it is well to ask one or more fathers to help make the viewer and the frames for the transparencies.

Turnover Pictures

Pictures are drawn or painted on large sheets of paper, at least 18″ x 24″ in size (white and colored newsprint in this size is available from school supply houses). When completed, they are attached to an easel or large piece of plywood and turned, one by one, as a description of each is given or as a script (perhaps created by those who prefer not to draw) is read.

Each child may make his own set of pictures depicting the events in the life of one of the persons studied in a unit, or each child may choose one portion of the study and make a picture that will become part of a set made by the class.

If the class wishes to do so, it can make the picture set into a large notebook as a permanent record of the study by binding it between two wood covers, hinged with leather strips.

Models

Primary and junior children enjoy molding clay into models of objects discussed in their study. If powdered clay is used, it will harden and can be painted after a few days. Children like to make villages (biblical, mission, or local), Palestinian household articles (lamps, water jugs, grinding stones, tables, and benches), and church furniture (altar, pulpit, baptismal font).

Upper juniors and junior-high young people enjoy carving soap or wax in making models. In a study of the history of the Christian church, one junior-high group designed an original symbol to represent each outstanding person in the church's story and then carved the symbols out of soap. A class of girls cut original symbols out of sheet copper, lacquered them to retard discoloration, and attached them to inexpensive chain bracelets. The symbols were not the traditional symbols of the church, but original symbols representing the great men of the church.

Relief Maps

Older children, who have studied geography, can have a good learning experience making a map. One kind is a relief map. A large sheet of plywood, coated with varnish, paint, or plastic to waterproof it, can be used as a base for a papier-mâché or flour-and-salt relief map.

Papier-mâché can be made by cutting newspaper into small pieces and soaking it in hot water, then boiling it for fifteen minutes. After cooling, the water is poured off and the pulp squeezed to remove excess water. To two cups of the pulp are added one cup of flour and one-half cup of salt. These are mixed thoroughly until they are like clay.

For flour-and-salt maps, equal parts of flour and salt are kneaded together with enough water added to make them stick together. Vegetable coloring may be added. If several colors are desired, the mixture can be divided into smaller parts and a different color kneaded into each. Both papier-mâché and flour-and-salt mixtures can be saved for later use by storing them in tightly covered containers.

The mixture is molded onto the base, following the outlines of rivers, lakes, and boundaries sketched with pencil. A week should be allowed for drying; then the map can be painted with tempera paints. For high mountains, it is best to use dry, crumpled newspaper covered with a layer of the mixture. The thin layer will dry much more quickly than a large mass of the mixture, and the map will be lighter in weight.

An easy way to make a large map according to accurate scale is to draw squares on the base and the same number of squares on the map which is being copied. One square at a time is reproduced on the larger map.

After the map has been painted, there are several possible variations in its use. Colored pins can be stuck into it at the points of interest, with an explanatory legend at the bottom. Pictures or symbols can be pasted on at appropriate places. Travels can be traced with yarn or string. Locations of significant events or people can be indicated with paper pennants attached to toothpicks. The names of cities, rivers, and other important places probably should be typed rather than printed, since the writing of most children is large. A child may do the typing.

Wall Maps

Unbleached muslin, a large sheet of wrapping paper, or a paper tablecloth can be used for making a good wall map. Crayon or tempera paint, or textile paint, in the case of muslin, may be used. A warm iron pressed over the crayon on muslin will set the colors. The method of enlarging described above may be used. A wall map can be made large enough to cover most of one wall of a classroom.

Translucent Map

A simple translucent map can be made by using tracing paper, parchment paper, lightweight silk, or oak tag board. After the map is completed, it is oiled with linseed oil and an electric light or flashlight is held behind it to illuminate a part of it softly. The light may be moved from one place to another to indicate places being discussed.

Time Line

A time line is a means of making graphic the chronology of events. Usually the time line represents a span of several centuries, with each century or half-century marked off. The names of significant persons and events are written at the appropriate spots along one side of the line, with pictures on the other side to represent those persons or events.

Since time lines have been used rather widely, it is well to try to find imaginative ways to make them.

One class used a rope for the time line, suspending it across one corner of the class space. Painted clothespins represented the century markings. Each week the class attached a symbol to the rope: a rock for Peter, a ship for Paul, a bird for St. Francis.

Another variation of the time line became a permanent fixture used by a class fortunate enough to have a room. It was used to help the children put into time sequence the events and people they studied. One wall was used for events before the time of Christ; another for events of the early church (first four centuries); a third for the fifth to nineteenth centuries; and the fourth for the twentieth century. A strip of wide wrapping paper was fastened around the room and the time chart was drawn on it. Even when the study did not call for it, members of the class found themselves turning to the proper wall to place in their minds the person or event being discussed.

Spatter Painting

Altar cloths, wall hangings, and notebook covers can be made by spatter painting. Cloth or paper can be used as the base. A pattern designed by the class (or gathered from nature, such as leaves) is pinned on the paper or cloth. Some groups use insect-spray guns to make the spatters, but most teachers prefer to use a slower method. Each child brings an old toothbrush and is given a small square of window screen tacked to a wooden frame. The toothbrush is dipped in washable ink, tempera paint, or white shoe polish (if a dark background is used). Each child practices, using a piece of paper and rubbing the toothbrush against the screen, held over the paper, until the spatters become fine and even. Then the toothbrush is rubbed against the screen immediately above the pattern and fine dots of color are sprayed over the background. When the paper or cloth is well covered with fine spatters and the ink or paint is dry, the pins and patterns are removed, leaving the design surrounded by colored spatter.

Children who have learned to make block letters in school enjoy making letters for an appropriate Bible verse to place on the background. More than one color of spatter can be used in a painting if desired.

Blueprint Pictures

Making blueprints is an interesting activity in units of study about God the Creator or about the beauty and orderliness of God's world. Children gather seeds, grass, ferns, and leaves that they wish to blueprint and press them between blotters under a weight.

Blueprint paper can be bought from architectural firms. It is best to ask for the kind that is set with water and that does not require a wash of potash. Each child needs a piece of cardboard, of blueprint paper, and of clear glass the size of the print desired. He places the blueprint paper on the cardboard, arranges on the blueprint paper the leaves or other objects to be printed, and lays the glass on top of it all to hold the paper and leaves flat. He places a few pieces of tape around the edges to hold the layers tightly together.

The material should be assembled indoors or under an umbrella to prevent turning of the blueprint paper. When ready, it is laid in the direct sunlight until the color of the paper turns. It is then taken back into the shade or indoors. The blueprint paper is removed and immediately put into a basin of clear water (or potash solution, depending on the type of paper used) to set the color. Then the picture is dried and can be mounted or framed. It is best that only a few children work on blueprints at one time.

Surprise Pictures

Kindergarten and primary children enjoy making surprise pictures. The teacher gives each child one thing: a piece of yarn, a leaf, a paper snowflake, a "pussy" from a pussy willow, or a bright piece of shiny paper. The child then makes a picture, using the thing the teacher gave him. A primary group had been talking about the wonders of the changing seasons and the signs of spring. The teacher gave each child a piece of yellow yarn. One child made a caterpillar, cocoon, and butterfly sequence; another made a kite string for a boy on a windy day; another made a spray of yellow flowers.

Giving the children something specific to work with is helpful to reticent members of the group, yet does not limit them. The many possibilities for using imagination is intriguing to the more creative members.

Service Activities

Junior and junior-high groups enjoy making something for someone else in the church. They can enamel nests of tin cans with gay colors for the nursery group. They collect cans ranging in size but all of the same height, carefully wash them, and inspect them to make sure there are no sharp edges. They then paint the cans with two coats of enamel. (Care should be taken to use only non-toxic enamel or paint.)

The preschool groups may need blocks that can be made by parents or young people and be sandpapered by juniors. The junior group may need a new cross, worship table, or hymnal bookcase. With careful planning to be sure that all the necessary materials and tools are available and that other groups will not be disturbed, a group can make this kind of construction activity very fruitful. It may be necessary to carry on the project during the week, and perhaps in the basement of a private home, to avoid disturbing other groups. Both the service rendered and the morale that develops in the class are worthwhile.

Figures

Children and young people make many kinds of figures for model villages, crèches, and dioramas, using material ranging from paper to wire and cloth. Directions for the more intricate ones are available in various books, such as those listed at the end of this chapter. Only one is described here, for which a clothespin base and paraffin-stiffened clothing are used.

A pipestem cleaner is wrapped just below the head of a conventional (non-spring type) clothespin to form the arms and is bent forward at the elbows. Modeling clay or powdered clay is molded around the top, to form the head, and around the pipestem cleaner to form the arms. The other end of the clothespin may be stuck in a flattened ball of clay as a base if desired. If the figure is to be Palestinian, a plain strip of cloth four inches wide and twelve inches long is used for the undergarment and a piece of striped cloth slightly narrower and eight inches long for the outer garment. A one-and-one-half-inch slit is cut in the plain cloth, along one side, one and one-half inches from each end and three inches farther from each end. This cloth is dipped in melted paraffin (melted in a coffee can floating in hot water, *not* over an open flame), allowed to drip for a moment over the can, then wrapped around the clothspin. It is best to start with one end at the back, gathering the material so that the first slit goes under one arm, the second one under the other arm, and on around the figure a second time, gathering the material so that the other two slits come under the two arms, ending at the back. The bottom of the garment is spread so that it hangs in folds. The work must be done quickly, as the paraffin dries rapidly. If the cloth stiffens too fast, it can be dipped again and the wrapping done over again.

A slit is then cut in the top edge of the outer garment one and one-half inches from each end. The cloth is dipped and allowed to drip. It is then placed around the figure, beginning at the center front and wrapped around once, ending at the front, with the top gathered so that the slits go under the arms. In the case of each garment, the top is pressed firmly to the figure.

When the paraffin dries, the figure stands by itself and is rich in appearance. A headdress is made by dipping a four-inch square of material in the paraffin and placing it in folds around the head, fashioned at the back of the head and shoulders, and with a band of contrasting material around the head to hold it in place.

If a larger figure is desired, a section of dowel rod can be used instead of a clothespin, with clothing materials correspondingly larger.

Since the paraffin hardens quickly, this activity should not be used with children younger than third-grade.

SOURCES OF OTHER IDEAS ON
CREATIVE ACTIVITIES

Adkins, George H., *Tools for Teachers* (St. Louis: The Bethany Press, 1962).

Beck, Ruth Armstrong, *Aim Your Activities at Teaching Religion* (New York: Office of P & D, National Council of Churches, 475 Riverside Drive).

Keiser, Armilda, *Here's How and When* (New York: Friendship Press, 1952).

Lobingier, Elizabeth M., *Activities in Child Education* (Boston: Pilgrim Press).

Rice, Rebecca, *Creative Activities* (Boston: Pilgrim Press).

XVII

The Use of
Creative Drama
with Children

"Let's get out of here!" shouted the sixth-grade boy playing Moses at the start of the Exodus, waving his arm. Although his statement lacked grammatical polish, the boy felt the slaves' need to escape and the urgency of his role as their leader. The group followed across the "Red Sea" without a smile. He had communicated with them.

Creative drama is a favorite activity of children because they make up their own dramatization. The material may be original or it may be based on a story that the group is studying. There is little or no scenery, costuming, or properties. The dialogue, because it grows out of immediate interaction, varies with each repetition. Emphasis is on free and spontaneous participation by as many children as possible rather than on acting excellence. The cast may be changed each time a scene is played, for all the children should be involved.

In creative drama the dialogue is usually original, as each

child attempts to respond to the situation as if he were actually the person he is playing. Children so genuinely enter into play-making that the activity often serves to draw together an otherwise disparate group. Imaginations are activated and esprit de corps grows remarkably.

The purpose of creative drama is not to present finished plays or even to teach a story in a more interesting way, but to help children get inside it by becoming the persons in it. The child's body and his feelings, as well as his mind, live through the experience of another person.

The Role of the Teacher

The imagination and sympathy of the teacher are important factors in encouraging children to express themselves in the roles of other persons. These faculties will help the members of the group to sharpen their eyes and ears to observe how people act when they are angry, sad, jealous, hurt, or happy. They will help create an atmosphere in which the children can try out walking, talking, sitting, and other actions as a person would perform them if he felt a certain way.

The teacher must help each child to develop the self-confidence needed to express his thoughts in front of his classmates and to gain the feeling that his contribution is important. He needs to encourage freshness of approach, originality, and independence of ideas. A reticent child often finds new trust in himself in a creative drama, if the evaluating comments are objective, if his hesitating and fragmentary efforts are appreciated seriously, and if he is allowed to grow at his own pace without criticism.

The teacher must help the group evaluate positively rather than negatively. Sometimes a hint about a more effective way to say or do something helps more than criticism. The teacher's own attitude of helpful appreciation will encourage the group to react to each member's efforts with understanding.

The teacher's role is not that of a "director of a play." Rather, he opens the door to creative experiences in drama for the children and is their companion in the venture, sharing in their feelings, their efforts to understand, their failure to make a character come alive, and their progress in feeling their way into the character until it lives for them.

Drama Without an Audience

Children enjoy making a play. They do not need an audience, for the joy of making the play is motivation enough. Dramatic activity comes to them as naturally as breathing, and an audience often induces self-consciousness, thereby making it impossible for the young actors to feel their way into the life of another person.

A group may wish to present its play for another group of children. An audience of children may respond vigorously, but they do not laugh or smile at the "cuteness" of the actors.

Choice of a Story to Be Dramatized

Not all stories can or should be dramatized. Some are more effective when read or told. A story that derives its beauty from descriptive passages, or that turns on thoughts rather than actions, is probably most effective when read. A story to be dramatized must have action and vivid dialogue. The people in it must be real rather than caricatures and the dialogue must be natural—to serve as a guide to the actors even though it is not reproduced verbatim. The story must appeal to the emotions. It must be worth the time and effort required to dramatize it. A trivial story, no matter how good its moral may be, is not worth working on, nor is one with a moralizing note at the end. Children can recognize the point of a story without having it pointed out.

Drama requires a climax. Children like a story that is "exciting," that has an economy of scenes, yet builds from one event to another and to the climax.

The teacher's own enthusiasm for a story helps children respond to it. The story must be well presented to the group. Generally it is better to tell it than to read it, because the mechanics of reading may get in the way of appreciation. However, if a teacher can read a story better than he can tell it, or if the story will lose richness of characterization or accuracy of dialogue in the telling, it should be read.

In telling a story for dramatization, direct discourse is more effective than indirect. Instead of "He asked his father for his share of the money," it is better to say, "He said, 'Father, I want my part of your money. Please give me my share.'"

Story Dramatization

Since children eight or more years old are capable of good characterizations, they should have a part in choosing the story to be dramatized. Talking over the story is one of the initial steps in working out the plans. Children must be able to visualize the story clearly before attempting to act it out. They need to hear it more than once. They need to understand the setting, plot, sequence of events, and characters. Hazy understanding will show up in fuzzy action and characterization.

The teacher needs to decide whether the children see the story with sufficient clarity. If they do not, he must devise some way of retelling the story, asking questions about what happened and why, whether it would make a good play and why, what characters are necessary, and what is important about each character.

The following questions may epitomize the steps to be taken in dramatizing a story: What scenes shall we include in making it into a play? What is a good starting place? What people do we need in the cast? Shall we play it through? How did we do, and how can we do it better?

Let us look at some of these questions in detail.

What Scenes Shall We Include?

In coming to a decision on this question, the group will consider what are the essential points of the story, which parts are the most important, and which might be deleted or combined. The teacher may write on the chalkboard the name of each scene that is proposed and a sentence about what should take place in it. After all the proposals have been made, the group must decide, with the teacher's help, whether some can be combined or need expansion. When the decision is final, the teacher will write the names of the scenes selected, as an outline for the group to follow.

What Is a Good Starting Place?

Since the opening scene must give the setting of the story, decisions should be made on these questions: Is the scene inside or outside? Where is the door (or window, or road)? What happens at the very first? How can we best portray these people?

One good way to begin the dramatization is to have each child try his hand at being a person prominent in the story. Several children may try it at the same time. For this initial "limbering up" it is not necessary to start at the beginning of the story. It may be better to choose a part of any scene that epitomizes the mood or feeling of the story and have the children portray it before starting to work on the rest of the dramatization.

What People Do We Need in the Cast?

If some of the scenes have been cut or expanded, the number of characters in the story may have to be changed. The teacher might write on the chalkboard the list of characters and, beside each character, something about him and the name of the child who will play the part. There may need to be more than one name opposite each character, as several children in succession should have the opportunity to play it.

Usually the children who volunteer to play the parts should be permitted to do so. Persuading children who are reluctant may make them all the more reticent and take the fun out of dramatizing the story. In asking for volunteers, the teacher should interpret the roles: "Who thinks he can act the way Albert Schweitzer felt when he was deciding to go to Africa?" The teacher should make sure that there are some capable, creative children in each scene. He will want to be aware, also, of the timid children who never volunteer, and will make it easy for them to take part without pushing them. After a scene has been played by two or three different casts, he may ask if everyone has had an opportunity to play a part, then include in the next cast those who have not participated.

Each role is talked about. "What kind of person is to be portrayed? How can we show what kind of person he is? How else could we show how he feels? If this happened to you, how would you feel, and what would you do or say to show how you feel?"

Shall We Play It Through?

Even with careful preparation, the first attempts will probably be rather rough and the teacher will need to exert much self-control to avoid giving too much direction. He should not interrupt to improve dialogue or grammar. If, however, he sees that a child does not have sufficient grasp of the story to carry his part, or if the whole cast seems unable to make the story move ahead, he should have the group stop and discuss the story again. Perhaps they have not done enough thinking or planning. The story may need to be retold or reviewed carefully. It may be that each character should be discussed a little more to make him "come alive" for the group.

If a child is overplaying or burlesquing a part, it is important for the teacher to indicate, kindly but firmly, that a play is dependent on the kind of actors it has. Each child must try very hard to be the person he is playing. If any child acts silly or "shows off," others forget who they are supposed to be and are unable to play their parts.

How Did We Do, and How Can We Do It Better?

After each group has played a scene, the class should evaluate the portrayal. The teacher can ask questions to stimulate constructive thinking about ways of changing and improving it. Questions that stimulate the children to think are more helpful than comments from the teacher. It may be necessary to recall the story and the characteristics of the persons portrayed. Often this helps the children to think of better ways to portray a person or a scene.

Sometimes a group will have difficulty thinking of ways to make the scene better. Instead of telling the class how to do it, the teacher should ask leading questions. "If you disagree with someone but feel that you cannot change his mind, what do you do and how do you feel? (Schweitzer's friends disagreed with his decision to become a doctor and go to Africa.)" "Can you think of ways to express Schweitzer's deep dismay when he returned to Africa after the First World War and found his hospital in ruins?" "Do you suppose the native workmen might stop work and look up for just a moment, letting us know for sure that they see Dr. Schweitzer?"

Sometimes a class responds enthusiastically to a wholly erroneous portrayal. In this case the teacher must gently lead the group to see that the person in the story was quite different. "What kind of person was the father in the Prodigal Son story? Was this the way the father was portrayed in the scene? Would you like to try again, Bill, now that we remember what the father was like?"

CREATIVE DRAMA FOR VARIOUS AGE GROUPS

Preschool Dramatic Play

A good share of the life of preschool children is spent in some kind of dramatizing activity: building a "big, big g'rage" out of blocks; taking the dolls for a walk to the store; playing mother and father in dress-up clothes; "spanking that bad boy" while punching a piece of soft clay; being a fire engine with all sirens open, rushing to put out a fire. Small children do not have to be taught dramatic play—they engage in it spontaneously, "trying on life."

Dramatic play is the real living out of which creative drama grows. It is not drama, for there is no beginning, end, climax, or plot. By means of dramatic play, children "try out" being a mother. They punish their children and love them, talk to them and scold them; they wash dishes and clothes, go to the grocery store, and talk to the father when he comes home. All these experiences are within the realm of the familiar. By means of dramatic play, children express the feelings and re-live the experiences that are a part of their lives.

A preschool child does not just push a truck across the floor; he becomes thereby a milkman, a mailman, or a fireman. "Look, teacher, I'm an airplane driver." "Hey, watch out for the fire truck. That house is on fire." "Look at me—I'm a giraffe with a big long neck."

Although young children usually need little or no encouragement from a teacher in dramatic play, some dramatizing experiences may not come to them without the teacher taking the initiative. For example, on an autumn day three- and four-year-olds have been making a collection of "fall wonders" on the wonder table. There are rocks and acorns, gourds and pumpkins, milkweed pods and thistles, and varicolored leaves. In the out-of-doors the children have watched fuzzy milkweed seeds float about in the breeze, and have helped them float by blowing at them. Now they are indoors, sitting on a rug.

The teacher says, "Would you like to hear a poem about the fuzzy little seeds we were playing with a few minutes ago?" The children nod enthusiastically, and the teacher recites a poem:

> In a milkweed cradle, snug and warm,
> Baby seeds are sleeping, safe from harm.
> Open wide the cradle, hold it high!
> Come, mister wind, come see them fly!

Then the teacher says, "Do you remember the way the little seeds were all curled up inside the pod like babies asleep, and how light and fuzzy thy were? What happened when you let them go into the wind?"

"They flew away."

"They flied up to the clouds."

"And some came back down."

"Mine tickled my nose."

"How would you like to play being milkweed seeds?" asks the teacher.

"Oo-oo-oh! Yes!"

"Can I be one? Can I be one?"

"How about the people on this side of the rug being the seeds, and those on that side being the wind?" After one "blow through," the sides change.

"How would it be," says the teacher, "if first we curled up tight inside the pod before it opened, like the seeds we saw that weren't fluffy yet? How about Dick, Jim, Suzie, and Sarah holding hands in a circle around the rest of the seeds to be the pod, then popping open their hands when the pod pops open?"

After a play-through, the teacher says, "Let's bow our heads and say a thank-you prayer for seeds and for wind that helps the seeds travel about."

There are many possibilities for simple informal dramatization by preschool groups. After an autumn trip to a woodland, the teacher might say, "Let's be colored leaves. Some of us will be red and some yellow. It is fall, and the wind is blowing." If the children are reticent or hesitant, he may suggest, "If you were a leaf on a tree and the wind blew so hard that you were blown away, you'd probably twirl around and around, wouldn't you, before you fell softly to the ground? I know a song about colored leaves that we can sing as we play we are leaves: 'Colored leaves, pretty leaves, falling from the trees, dancing in the breeze, whirling in the breeze.'"

Another time little curled-up bodies represent brown bulbs in the ground. Some children "rain" gently on them, other children "shine" on them, and others "snow" quietly, making a blanket for them. Slowly, something begins to happen to the hard brown bulbs. The little bodies uncurl as the bulbs push up green sprouts through the earth. Arms reach up, heads look up, and radiant faces between uplifted hands announce that a flower has blossomed from the once dead-appearing bulbs.

On a snowy Sunday the children have watched the snow swirling by the window, and may even have gone out to feel it on their tongues and watch it on their coats. The teacher asks them to listen to find out whether the snowflakes make any noise. Then the group is transformed into a noiseless swirl of snowflakes as the teacher sings, "The snowflakes are blowing, whirling, and twirling, silently covering the ground."

Now and then in these dramatizing activities, the teacher may have to make a suggestion, but no effort should be made to produce a finished creation. The joy is in the being and doing—the "trying out" of life. A teacher can see that there is the proper climate for children to engage in dramatic play: freedom, an unhurried pace, child-size equipment and surroundings, and responsive adults.

School-Age Drama Experiences

Five- and six-year-olds are likely to continue in the same pattern of dramatic play as three- and four-year-olds. The stories they enjoy most are about things they know, with characters who are like people they know. Older children, unless they have imaginative teachers who help them continue with dramatizing activities, may become self-conscious about it. Seven- and eight-year-olds are becoming interested in remote people and things. They enjoy fantasy as well as reality, and they like longer stories. The nativity story is a favorite for dramatizing. These children especially enjoy puppet and shadow plays with narration.

Nine-, ten-, and eleven-year-olds respond to hero stories and to realistic action, although they also enjoy humor. The story of Joseph and his brothers is excellent for this age group, for it has a strong and interesting plot, vivid action, opportunities for dialogue, varied characters, and emotional appeal. The favoritism, jealousy, anger, and love in this story are strong feelings that these children know. The stories of the Good Samaritan and the Prodigal Son also have possibilities, as has the nativity story.

Twelve-, thirteen-, and fourteen-year-olds enter into rituals and ceremonies. They like mystery, suspense, and excitement, together with some idealism. Incidents from the lives of great contemporary men, such as Gordon Seagrave (the Burma Surgeon), Albert Schweitzer, Toyohiko Kagawa, and others, are useful, as well as the stories of Bible characters such as Moses, Paul, and Stephen.

A church school class in its dramatizing activities has a disadvantage that public school or vacation school classes do not have. It is difficult to have carry-over with a week's gap between sessions. Yet, if interest is high and the whole class is involved, this obstacle may be overcome. The children may want to come early to work on the play. Primary and younger children probably want to repeat what they did the week before, but it is difficult for them to build a continuing, cumulative experience. Children in the junior and junior-high departments, however, are capable of sustaining interest over several weeks. Work on a play should not last more than six to eight weeks. After that period most juniors are ready to move on to something new.

One point about dramatizing activities must be emphasized. The important element is the children's involvement in "trying on" another person's experiences. As the child grows in this skill, whether through drama, pantomime, puppetry, interviews, or radio plays, he should be given opportunity and encouragement to formulate his own way of saying things. His speaking may be crude, but he can learn with practice to be more polished and free. He will find this difficult if he is tied to reading a script which the teacher has prepared. A teacher may be tempted to write out dialogue and have children learn or read it, but this does not give them the experience of formulating their own responses.

Pantomime

Pantomime is a good starter activity with older children, especially with those who have not had much experience in dramatization. Pantomime gives self-conscious or unsure children a chance to try out actions with the body without having to speak. Emphasis is on inner feeling, natural movements, and the way people look and act. The group may talk, for instance, about how a man is likely to move when he is angry. Then they try out being persons in an anger-producing situation to see whether their actions actually communicate anger.

Feeling is important in pantomime. There is a striking difference between the pantomime of a boy woodenly washing the supper dishes, and of a boy washing the dishes while the ball team waits under the kitchen window, his mother having threatened to withdraw his allowance if the dishes are not washed. The latter has tension and conflict, and therefore drama.

The incident of Jesus dealing with the money-changers in the temple, for example, has many possibilities for creative drama because of its action and the interplay of strong feelings. If it is used, half the group might try being Jesus and the other half the money-changers. Later, other characters can be added. The drama is more interesting and more easily pantomimed if the individual sellers and money-changers are given characteristics— slyness, greediness, pride, self-righteousness, or bombast. Some state of feeling might be assigned to each of the disciples—some reacting in fear, some in surprise, some in dismay.

Puppetry

The use of simple puppetry with second-grade and older children makes an interesting variation in play-making. There is anonymity in puppetry that pleases children who do not like to appear in front of others, even their own classmates. Most children are enthusiastic about a puppet show and about creating their own puppets.

The show may be done very simply by manipulating the puppets along the edge of a table, from behind it, or more elaborately by creating a stage in which the puppets act. The top of the piano is also a good place for a show, because the piano hides the manipulators. The amount of class time required for making puppets may be cut considerably by asking each child (with his parents' help) to make and robe a puppet at home. In a note to the mother, the teacher can indicate who the puppet is supposed to be and some characteristics of his dress, and give instructions for making it.

The possibilities of spontaneous and creative dialogue are the same in a puppet play as in informal dramatization. A disadvantage is that there is less opportunity to experiment with the way feelings affect bodily movements. However, some teachers consider this an advantage, especially for children who have had no experience with informal drama. The children can concentrate on what they (or the puppets) are going to say.

The steps in creating a puppet play and in acting out a story are almost identical, except that additional time must be allowed for the construction of the puppets. The questions suggested in the section "Story Dramatization," above, are appropriate as a guide.

Following are a few kinds of puppets that can be made and used in church school. The ones suggested are simple because of the limitations of time in church school.

1. *Paper-bag puppets.* A small paper bag is fitted over a child's hand and down to the wrist. The child puts his first three fingers together, with the thumb and little finger spread. The three fingers are the head of the puppet, the thumb and little finger the arms. The teacher should squeeze the paper around the three fingers and around the thumb and the little finger. The neck and arms of the puppet can be held in place with a piece of string tied around each loosely so that the puppet can be removed easily. The play can be done without any details of face, hair, or costume on the puppet, or the children can add facial details and costuming by drawing on the paper with crayon. Cloth robes, as well as beards and hair of yarn, may be added.

2. *Cloth-mitten puppets.* These are similar to paper-bag puppets in shape and simplicity. The teacher traces onto cloth a three-section mitten the appropriate size to fit the child's hand. The center section, large enough for three fingers, is the head; the two smaller sections are the arms. Each child cuts two pieces of cloth and sews them together with a whip stitch, leaving the bottom open for slipping on the hand. The children talk about the kind of people these puppets represent and then color them

with crayons. Taping the mitten to the table during the coloring prevents it from slipping.

3. *Hand puppets.* Although hand puppets require a longer time to complete, many older children and their teachers prefer them because of their durability. They can be used to dramatize different stories by adding a sash or cap to change the character. A hand-puppet head is molded on the end of a stick or a cardboard cylinder, with a piece of cloth large enough to cover the child's hand serving as the puppet's robe. The head is molded from some pliable material, such as wallpaper cleaner, papier-mâché, flour-and-salt mixture, or clay. It can be painted with tempera paints after it has dried for a week. If the cardboard cylinder is used, the operator can insert his middle fingers into it. Arms can be added in the robe and be operated by the thumb and little finger. If papier-mâché is used as material for the head, it is well to plan a weekday session to prepare the material, or have it already cooked and prepared before class time.

An interesting variant of hand puppets is made as follows: Make a cone of cardboard six to eight inches high for the body of the puppet, leaving the smaller end with an opening large enough to receive the neck of a light bulb. Use a small light bulb as the head. Dip pieces of old sheeting in a thin solution of plaster of Paris. Pull tightly over the head and insert into the small end of the cone, smoothing the face free of wrinkles. Drape other pieces around the cone for robes. The plaster hardens, with permanent pleats and folds wherever draped. The dried robe and face may be painted with tempera. Since the plaster makes the robes stiff, the figures will stand alone and may also be used for dioramas.

4. *Sock puppets.* A darning-cotton spool is used as the foundation for the head of the puppet, with the toe of a white cotton sock tied over it. Facial features can be added with pencil, crayon, or embroidery. The spool is then attached to a stick or cylinder to make the puppet figure.

5. *Finger puppets.* Children enjoy the variation of making finger puppets instead of hand puppets. The directions are the same except that the cylinder used as the base of the puppet is small enough to fit over one finger only, and the costume is, accordingly, tiny.

6. *Shadow puppets.* A committee of children, with one or two fathers, can meet during the week to build the shadow-puppet stage, eliminating the necessity of using church school time for construction. A frame is built about four feet wide, shaped like the proscenium of a stage, to rest either on its own legs or on a table. A piece of white cloth is stretched tight to fill the opening. A floodlight is placed on a table back of the stage at a distance to make a sharp shadow on the cloth when the puppets are placed behind it. If the cloth is stretched on a light frame that can be inserted in the stage opening, it can be removed when the stage is to be used for other puppets.

Shadow puppets are made by cutting silhouette figures out of cardboard and attaching them with thumbtacks to sticks. It is well to call the children's attention to distinguishing characteristics of the persons in the story—one may be fat, one skinny, one may have a plume on his hat—so that the shadow of each can be distinguished from those of the others.

Dramatized Interviews

Closely related to, but not identical with, informal dramatization is the "interview." Rather than making a play out of the story, the group dramatizes an interview with a person they have studied.

The group discusses the life and qualities of the person, making a list of his accomplishments and characteristics on the chalkboard. A variety of situations can be used as settings for interviews: the person might be on a television variety program; he might appear as a guest on a radio program; he might call a press conference; or a newspaper reporter might interview him to do an article about him. After deciding on the kind of interview, the group needs to talk about what a reporter interviewing the person would want to know.

"Now," says the teacher, "who would like to interview St. Francis of Assisi? Who would like to be St. Francis (or Moses, Peter, David, Abraham, Amos)? Let's try it out."

A variation of this approach is for the teacher to be the interviewer and each class member in turn to be St. Francis or another person interviewed. The teacher goes from one to another, asking questions. When the interview is finished, the class considers whether the interviewer and the person interviewed were in character, and suggests improvements.

Radio Plays

A radio play has some of the advantages of puppetry in introducing dramatizing activities or in varying them. The emphasis is on dialogue. Groups with cramped quarters or in a room which provides little privacy find the radio play a good medium.

The process is much the same as that for making a story into a play. The original story should have considerable suspense, active characterizations, and lively dialogue possibilities. The class must have the story clearly in mind; they need to talk about the scenes and people to be included and the best way of beginning. An announcer is needed. Some commercials might be interjected now and then for fun. A tin-can microphone with class call letters on it adds to the atmosphere, as do signs saying "Silence" or "On the Air."

All children who wish it should be given the opportunity to try being each character. Though there are no set lines, a great deal of discussion must precede any attempt to play the story. Some classes have enjoyed tape-recording a radio play, using the children who gave the best portrayals.

Original plays

Dramatizing is usually most satisfactory when children use as the basis for a play a story that is already written, rather than attempting to create their own story. The process of making up a story is time-consuming, and the results usually are so crude and artless that the story is not worth dramatizing. It is best to use stories by skillful writers.

There are groups and situations, however, in which it may be helpful to create original drama. The following are some examples: (1) The group may look at a picture portraying a problem or an action situation, then make up a brief dramatic episode about it. (2) After studying a Bible story or the life of a great man, the class can dramatize another ending to the story, or an imaginary event in the man's life. (3) The group may dramatize a present-day version of a Bible story they have studied, after talking about where and how a similar situation might occur today. (4) The teacher tells an "open-ended" story—one that ends with the situation unresolved. The group must decide what happens next and how to end the story. Dramatizing is a good way of trying out various alternate endings of the story.

SUMMARY

Dramatizing activities can be a most interesting and effective avenue of learning. By recreating and living in the roles of other persons we can learn from those persons by participating in their experiences. It is as if we view the lives of persons from the inside, sympathetically and with understanding, entering into their struggles, disappointments, hopes, and achievements. In the process we come to know them much more intimately than when we only hear about them.

Note: The authors are especially indebted to Winifred Ward and her excellent book, *Playmaking With Children* (New York: D. Appleton-Century-Crofts, Inc., 1947). Persons wishing to use creative drama with older children and young people will find help in another book by the same author and publisher, *Creative Dramatics for Upper Grades and Junior High School.*

Epilogue

Some readers of this book may wonder whether it does not propose responsibilities for the teacher that no person should be asked to carry. Yet, Christian education must be more vigorous than it is pictured in these pages, rather than less vigorous, if it is to meet the needs of children and young people. No one of the groups described, nor its leaders, would claim that they did enough, or as much as they wanted to do. Christian education must be imaginative, experimental, hopeful—reaching for answers to pressing, urgent needs.

In Christian education we must face the fact that the great questions about the meaning of life and about reasons for Christian faith come to children and young people at a much earlier age than used to be the case. Terrific pressures bear upon children and young people today. A world of strife, prejudice, mobility, and threat poses questions about what really is worthful and permanent—worth giving a life to.

Vocational choices force young people to make hard decisions. Most young people used to inherit a life work—on the farm, in the store, in father's office. Today the range of occupational choices is fabulous. With the lure of fantastic salaries, automation, flights around the earth and to the moon, ever deeper probing into the make-up of the universe—in such a rapidly moving world, where do ultimate values come in, and what is their claim on children and young people?

There are no pat, easy answers, and children and young people soon come to know it. Our grappling along with them in the great mysteries of the known and unknown must be honest, intelligent, and aggressive. Christian education must be much more than lecturing to classes or telling stories about things that happened 2,000 years ago. Unless the validity of Christianity in the lives of families and their children and young people today can be discovered, we can talk endlessly and accomplish no real Christian learning.

Teachers in the church must face the demands of their task squarely and honestly. Christian education must be the most we can make it, not the easiest and the least. Teachers must have a positive, growing faith of their own to share. That faith must be won in the wrestling with God's revelation of himself through the Holy Spirit of today as well as in the Christ of nearly 2,000 years ago. It comes through seeking, studying, praying, sharing, and re-examination.

These pages are not presented as giving easy or final answers to questions about teaching the Christian faith. They are written in the hope that teachers who want to go along with children and young people in the venture of Christian faith and living will find some reassurance and inspiration in them. Nothing can bring more joy than, as parent or teacher, being the companion of a child or young person as life's meaning under God is opened to him.